Country Roads
~ of the ~
MARITIMES

A Guide Book
from Country Roads Press

Happy Birthday mom
I hope you enjoy your
trip to the east coast,
this might help.   -greg
                June 28 1998

Country Roads
~ of the ~
MARITIMES

New Brunswick, Prince Edward Island, and Nova Scotia

Judith Comfort

Illustrated by
Victoria Sheridan

Country Roads Press
CASTINE • MAINE

**Country Roads of the Maritimes: New Brunswick,
Prince Edward Island, and Nova Scotia**
© 1994 by Judith Comfort. All rights reserved.

Published by Country Roads Press
P.O. Box 286, Lower Main Street
Castine, Maine 04421

Text and cover design by Edith Allard
Illustrations by Victoria Sheridan
Typesetting by Camden Type 'n Graphics

ISBN 1–56626–045–X

Library of Congress Cataloging-in-Publication Data

Comfort, Judith.
    Country roads of the Maritimes : New Brunswick, Prince
Edward Island, and Nova Scotia / Judith Comfort ; illustrator,
Victoria Sheridan.
        p.   cm.
    Includes bibliographical references and index.
    ISBN 1–56626–045–X : $9.95
    1. Maritime Provinces—Guidebooks.   2. Automobile
travel—Maritime Provinces—Guidebooks.   I. Title.
    F1035.8.C7   1994
    917.1504′4–dc20   93–44946
                                                                  CIP

Printed in the United States of America.
10 9 8 7 6 5 4 3 2 1

For Ruthie, my navigator and travelling companion

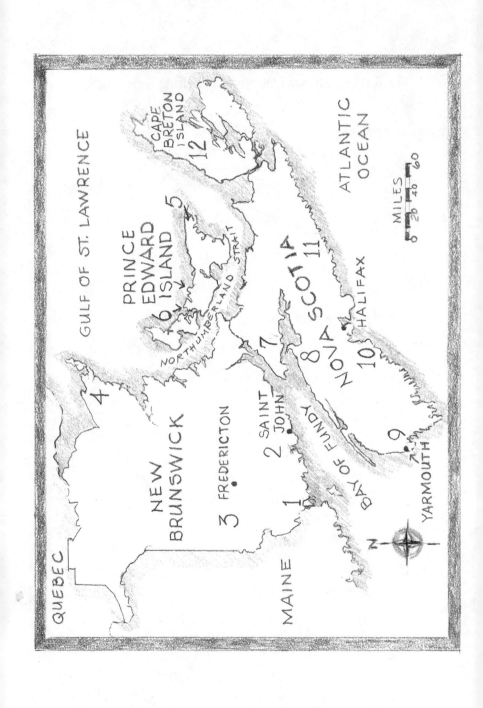

Contents

(& Key to the Maritimes' Country Roads)

Introduction

Before heading out on the back roads of the Maritime Provinces I appeared on our local CBC "Radio Noon" phone-in show. I explained to listeners a little about my project, and they were asked to call in with their recommendations for where I should travel. I carefully noted their comments but was not prepared for the strong emotion with which people spoke.

One woman called in to tell us about Minister's Island, near St. Andrews, New Brunswick. Her parents had been brought out from England to tend the gardens of the Van Horne estate on the island. She was carried across the inlet as a newborn, but she commented that if her mother had had her way, she would have been born right on the island. Her childhood and this beautiful island are inextricably tied together.

A soft-spoken gentleman with a Gaelic lilt called in to talk about a Cape Breton glen where his parents and grandparents are buried.

Another man described how he finds himself returning again and again to Advocate Harbour, where the beach is littered with a tangle of seaweed and driftwood deposited by the tumultuous Fundy tides.

When I headed out to explore the country roads of the Maritimes I did not know what I would find. In retrospect I now know that it had been spelled out very clearly by the callers to the show. The subject of every single call was the unspoiled natural beauty of the Maritimes.

I was awed by harbours and valleys and forests of extraordinary beauty. The problem was how to describe, in words, these settings that left me speechless.

My family and I have lived on the edge of a tiny beach on Medway Harbour for twenty years. We swim here in the summer, pick mussels off the rocks, but more than anything, we gaze out at it. As constant as our kitchen table is the view out the window, which we absorb as we linger over a cup of coffee every morning. In the evening we stare at the great blue herons silhouetted in the setting sun.

To me, this beach has always been called, well—the beach. This book has forced me to discover a whole new vocabulary: barrier beaches and sand spits, tombolos, rubble, and my favourite—probably because of the delicious sound of the words—swash and backwash. In attempting to describe Cherry Hill Beach, a rough and ragged crescent of sand across the harbour from "my" beach, I discovered an interesting phenomenon that I had never noticed in dozens of visits before. The smell and sound of the beach hit me long before I laid eyes on it. I was forced to look at the familiar with fresh eyes.

If trying to describe even this minute corner of my life was such a challenge, writing about three whole provinces was a humbling experience. It wasn't just the fact that I was writing about such a powerful subject, but also that I was writing about other people's beaches. How could I begin to interpret the hundreds or even thousands of years of human experience associated with each place?

Much to my regret, I could not visit every square mile of the Maritimes or even a fraction of the shoreline. I apologize for what I have left out; it is there to be discovered without my assistance. The best guides to travelling are undoubtedly the people who are rooted in the places we visit, the people with a deep uncompromising passion for the land.

NEW BRUNSWICK

©1994 V. SHERIDAN

1 ~

Island Hopping:

Campobello, Deer Island, and St. Andrews by-the-Sea

From Calais, Maine: Travel south on US 1 about 33 kilometres (20 miles) to Whiting, then turn left on State 189 east to Lubec. Follow the signs through the town to the bridge to Campobello Island and the Canadian border. This trip traverses two islands and 33 kilometres (20 miles) of coastline across the top of Passamaquoddy Bay, ending at St. Andrews. Travel time without stops: one day.

Highlights: *Passamaquoddy Bay, Campobello Island, the Roosevelt summer home, a ferry ride, Deer Island, Old Sow Whirlpool, aquacultured salmon, herring weirs, the Atlantic Salmon Centre, St. Andrews, historic architecture, Greenock Presbyterian Church, "watering place of the Dominions," the Algonquin Hotel, Vincent Massey School playground, Covenhoven.*

High up on the arched Franklin Delano Roosevelt International Memorial Bridge, crossing Lubec Narrows from Maine, U.S.A., to Campobello Island, Canada, we get our first glimpse of the Quoddy River and islands.

River is a curious term to apply to this saltwater channel whose banks are defined only by island bluffs. *Narrows* and *passages* would more accurately describe the waterways in this area where swift currents between rocks, combined with temperamental tides, must be negotiated by mariners with extreme caution.

Our tour takes us over bridges, on ferries, and on roads around the Canadian perimeter of what is affectionately called the "Quoddy Loop." Passamaquoddy Bay is the salt-water heart of a fascinating landscape. It is bounded on the east by the state of Maine and the St. Croix River, which defines the international border between Canada and the United States. Jutting into the water from the northern edge are fingers of land. At the tip of the most prominent peninsula is St. Andrews, New Brunswick. To the southeast, Passa-maquoddy is virtually cordoned off from the wild waters of the Bay of Fundy by a fascinating archipelago. The islands, ledges, rocks, and nubs stretch from Lubec, Maine, to Blacks Harbour, New Brunswick.

Just off the Roosevelt Bridge is a friendly customs officer and a sign that reads, "Welcome/Bienvenu New Brunswick." One hundred metres (330 feet) straight ahead is the tourist bureau. Exploring an island is different from puttering around the mainland (there aren't that many options for leaving!), so it's a good idea to stop here for advice.

The staff is quick with a yellow pen and can highlight on a map the golf course, beaches, and hiking trails on the island. But what we really need help with is the timing of our trip. When does the ferry leave Campobello for Deer Island? How long does the crossing take? Can we make it to St. Andrews tonight? If we fall in love with Campobello, how do we make reservations to spend the night?

The bureau staff points most people in the direction of Roosevelt Cottage, the former summer home of Eleanor and Franklin Delano Roosevelt and now the centre point of an international park.

Campobello is synonymous in most people's minds with the Roosevelt family, and their summer home is, deservedly, the focal point for most visitors to the island.

The kitchen at the Roosevelt Cottage, Campobello

At the entrance, one of the first things we see is a birch-bark canoe mounted on the wall. Next to it is a large-as-life photograph of FDR as a young and strikingly handsome man commandeering the very same canoe. Artifacts like this breathe life into history throughout the house.

The thirty-four-room "cottage" has been completely restored, from the copper water boiler in the kitchen to the polished wooden parlor floors and the canvas swing on the verandah. There is a palpable joyful presence here, not only to be found in the photographs of laughing children, but in the serene ambience of the rooms. The guides urge us on, but we want to linger in the rooms and absorb the details of domestic life in days gone by.

It's easy to imagine Eleanor and Franklin Delano Roosevelt relaxing over their books in the living room. Supper is ready, they step out onto the porch to summon, with the help of a megaphone, the children who come racing across the lawn.

Simply put, the place does not feel like a museum. It is more like the home of a dear friend. Finding other visitors on tour through the house is not a distraction. In fact, it adds a liveliness that must have been a main ingredient of the atmosphere here when the fourteen bedrooms were teeming with guests.

Leaving the park, we stick to the tried-and-true paths of Campobello—the marked roadways of the international park and the adjacent provincial park (especially Herring Cove Beach, considered to be the nicest beach on the island, offering a grand view of the high cliffs of Grand Manan Island). The shoreline beyond the park limits is inaccessible by car. Much of the original forest has been cut over and there are extensive bogs.

The ferry to Deer Island operates out of Welshpool from the last week in June to Labour Day. A hand-stenciled sign marks the entrance to a short gravel road that breaks through the willow shrubs down to the pebble beach. There is no ferry terminal, no wharf, ramp, or toll gate. The system is plain and simple.

A barge with a small boat attached to the side approaches the beach. A ramp flaps down and half a dozen cars drive onto the sand, through the trees, and up to the road.

Gently, we are coaxed onto the barge. Then we are instructed to inch our cars forward to readjust the weight—so the barge can get off the beach. A little way out, the tug detaches, turns itself around, and, facing the open water, steams away from Campobello.

On a fine summer day, this forty-five-minute ride may very well be the highlight of our whole journey. Everyone gets out of their car to enjoy the warm breezes. The surf froths up like bubble bath between the cracks in the plate steel platform, making the children giggle. Passengers note the license plates of fellow travellers and, before the end of the ride, have swapped the names of mutual acquaintances and notes on the area.

Close to Deer Island, the surface of the water breaks up into a curious myriad of eddies, tide rips, and whirlpools. The largest of the whirlpools is called the "Old Sow." When the tide is just right, three hours prior to high tide (especially during the new and full moons) the Sow is 9 metres (30 feet) in diameter and 1.2 metres (4 feet) deep. At off times she breaks up into a number of smaller whirlpools. (Someone suggested that they should be called "piglets.")

A good place to study the whirlpools on land is at Island Point, on Deer Island, close to the beach where we leave the ferry. The ferry offloads its passengers and we head north to Lambertville to catch another ferry that will take us from Deer Island to Letete, on the mainland.

The road is wooded, with breaks at Chocolate Cove, Leonardville, Northwest Harbour, and Lords Cove. Any of these tiny coves would be a good place to settle in for a few days. The giant shade trees and generous porches are welcoming. There are numerous bed and breakfasts and camping at Deer Island Point at Lords Cove and all kinds of wild blackberries. (Pick them only when they are coal black and juicy.)

The mainstay of this island is the fishery. Deer Island boasts the largest lobster pound in the world, featuring floating pens and rafted boxes that store one million pounds of live lobster.

Also a going concern here is the aquaculture of salmon. Next to rocks and ledges are hundreds of yellow buoys attached to mesh cages of swimming fish. This is a serious business. Salmon are nurtured with highly specialized feed containing food dyes and antibiotics, dispensed at scientifically regulated times. By 1995, the aquacultured salmon industry is predicted to be worth $100 million to New Brunswick.

At Leonardville a stone breakwater snakes across the water from Bar Island. We pull off the road to look at the complex community of boats, trucks, and peculiar floating platforms.

The platforms, or scows, are seats for pile drivers that pound long stakes into the ocean floor. Hundreds of stakes are pounded to form fences that trap fish. These traps are called weirs (pronounced "wares"). They are traditionally shaped like a balloon on the end of a stick. Herring (and unfortunately the odd tuna and porpoise) are funnelled into the trap and then have difficulty escaping because the mouth of the weir is turned inward. The school of fish swims in circles until a fisherman enters at low tide, gathers them together in a net, and pumps them out with a hydraulic vacuum hose.

The best weir sites are at the extreme ends of points of land and in channels between two or more islands or ledges. For this the Passamaquoddy region, including the eastern side of Deer Island, is perfectly suited.

The ferry from Deer Island to Letete is considerably more substantial than the Campobello-Deer Island ferry. Operated by the provincial government, it is free of charge. The boat carefully picks its way through the intimate narrows, making for a beautiful but noisy cruise except for when they (thank goodness) cut the engine to make a ninety-degree turn.

Follow Route 772 east for 11.6 kilometres (7 miles) to St. George and pick up Route 1 west toward Calais and St. Stephen. Unfortunately there is no scenic alternative to the main road between Saint John and the American border. Travel for 12 more kilometres (7 miles) until the corner just past Digdeguash. Turn left on Route 127 to St. Andrews and drive for about 17 more kilometres (10 miles). This overland route takes us over 33 kilometres (20 miles) of road, which a seagull could do in a mere 8 kilometres (5 miles) or so, soaring across the bay.

Halfway between Bocabec and St. Andrews is Chamcook, home of the Atlantic Salmon Information and Visitor Centre, which is the international headquarters of the Atlantic Salmon Federation. Its mandate is to restore the natural salmon population, which has been damaged by pollution and overfishing. As part of its program to educate the public, the Federation opened the centre in 1988 on Chamcook Creek.

Inside, the posters and printed materials are educational, but we'd rather be outside in the cedar woods watching the baby salmon. They live in small nursery tubs that are gravity-fed by the babbling creek. A mesh cover protects them from bird predators. This is an experimental way of raising fish, at the natural creek site rather than miles away in a hatchery.

Farther down the creek, mature fish swim in a large pool in the creek bed. A shed has been constructed next to the pool, and in the basement room children pressing their noses against the glass can observe the salmon eyeball to eyeball.

Back on Route 127 to St. Andrews we head for the Welcome Centre, a large, beautiful home on Reed Avenue. This town has been catering to tourists for over 100 years, and there are lots of things to do in the area: whale watching, golfing, and pottery classes at the Sunbury Shores Art and Nature

Centre, to name a few. The Huntsman Marine Laboratory and Aquarium is close by, and we find supervised swimming at Katy's Cove. The town has many times more crafts and gift shops, restaurants, and accommodations than similar Maritime towns of its size.

It's essential to pick up a copy of the St. Andrews map and directory. With it, finding your way around town will be as easy as making the moves on a Monopoly board.

The old pioneer town, laid out by British army surveyors, was a grid pattern of sixty perfectly square blocks. The streets were named for members of the royal family of King George III: Harriet, Mary, Adolphus, Elizabeth, Edward, William, King, Frederick, Princess Royal, Sophia, Ernest, Augustus, and Patrick.

This British sense of order was meant to provide a secure haven for the newly arrived settlers, who were citizens of the Thirteen Colonies who wished to remain loyal to the Crown after the ferment of the American Revolution.

Many of them had left cultured, urban lifestyles in New York and Massachusetts to start a new life. They moved to what they thought was the British side of the new international border, the Penobscot River. Many were involved in the military establishment at Fort George and built homes at Castine, Maine. Unfortunately for them, the border was moved to the St. Croix River and the United Empire Loyalists were forced to make a second pilgrimage, this time to St. Andrews.

In 1783, 640 men, women, and children arrived by ship, with everything they owned in the world, including their newly constructed homes hewn from the Maine woods. An additional 125 men and their families, from the Argyll Highlanders stationed at Fort George, took their discharge here rather than be returned to Scotland.

Within five years, 600 buildings were constructed. Today, according to *The St. Andrew's Heritage Handbook*, "48% of the structures in the original town plot have been lived in for more than 100 years and many are nearing the 200 mark." We picked up a copy of this book, published by St. Andrews Civic Trust, at Blue Peter Books. It describes in detail the different architectural styles of the community.

The book is a good walking guide. Photographs illustrate a stately Georgian home, built in 1784, on Water Street, a Cape Cod on Queen Street, and many more.

For a guide to domestic and public buildings, the Civic Trust publishes a pamphlet called *A Guide to Historic St. Andrews* that describes churches, cemeteries, museums, the courthouse, and the registry office.

The Greenock Presbyterian Church at the corner of Edward and Montague Streets is of interest because of the superb craftsmanship that went into its construction. Built in 1824, it is said to be one of the most beautiful and most costly churches in New Brunswick. Ten solid pillars of locally grown bird's-eye maple support the gallery, which is trimmed with imported solid mahogany. The pulpit rises in two stages to the gallery and was put together entirely without nails. The design for the pulpit is based on one that existed in Greenock, Scotland, birthplace of Capt. Christopher Scott, who was the main financial contributor to the church.

Another architectural era coexists with the Loyalist buildings. Included are over fifty architect-designed, ofttimes mammoth, summer homes of the rich and famous.

In the 1870s St. Andrews was described by one Saint John newspaper as the "Watering Place of the Dominions." Two fathers of the Confederation, Sir Leonard Tilley and Sir Charles Tupper, had summer cottages here. The community, sensing the potential economic benefits of tourism, lobbied for better rail service and hotel accommodations. In 1872, the railway linking Saint John and Maine was completed, making it possible to travel from Boston to St. Andrews in less than twenty-four hours.

The Algonquin Hotel, which opened its doors in 1889, was pivotal in the development of St. Andrews as a summer haven. VIP guests came by special Pullman cars to the grand opening and included the governor-general of Canada, Lord Stanley, and the governor of Maine. The prime minister, Sir John A. MacDonald, and Lady MacDonald unfortunately couldn't make it but did come down for a visit soon after the opening.

As a sign of the times, one of the main conveniences of the hotel, which the proprietor saw fit to mention in his first advertisement, was the "drainage by perfect sewers, having an average descent of 7 1/2%," which "falls directly into the sea 2000 feet distant." This modern establishment boasted "ladies' and gentleman's toilet rooms on each floor."

The Algonquin Hotel is a landmark of its era and is worth a drive past even if a stay is not in the budget. Imagine that you are there in 1910, stepping out of the carriage, walking under the archway and through the grand entrance, to be greeted with baskets of fresh flowers and a kilted piper.

The area around the Algonquin includes mansion after mansion, wrought-iron fences, hedges, and gardeners busily weeding flower beds.

In the midst of this is a wonderful children's playground, across from the Vincent Massey School. (We were lucky enough to be travelling with our children, who could take advantage of the ropes, mazes, monkey bars, stages, picnic tables, plastic pipe organs, periscope, tire swings, and kaleidoscope.)

The playground is a work of art. The wooden structure includes a seashell mosaic created by the local children and medieval spires that mimic the Algonquin Hotel. Professionally designed, the playground was constructed in a few days entirely with volunteer help. The materials for the playground were purchased with money left by the Olive Hosmer Trust. Miss Hosmer was the owner of Linden Grange, Sir

Samuel Leonard Tilley's home on Edward and William Streets. She died childless in 1965 and left money in her will to provide playgrounds and sports fields for the children of St. Andrews.

For a detailed description of the summer "cottages" we recommend a book called *No Hay Fever and a Railway: Summers in St. Andrews, Canada's First Seaside Resort* by Willa Walker. Most of the homes in Ms. Walker's book are privately owned but there is one fascinating place that is open to the public.

Covenhoven, the 600-acre estate of Sir William Cornelius Van Horne, founder of the Canadian Pacific Railway, is located on Minister's Island. Because of the amazing tides in this part of the world and because of the hard pebble bottom of the channel, cars drive on the ocean floor across to the island.

The Province of New Brunswick has owned the property since 1982. Restoration, however, is not complete, and tours of the houses and grounds are available only on a limited basis, depending on the time of year, and of course the tides. It's best to inquire at the tourist bureau for details.

To get to Minister's Island, follow the Bar Road just past the Algonquin golf course to the shore. If the time is right, boats will be sitting high and dry in the muck and the weirs will be empty.

A sign clearly states the safe crossing times: "At high tide the bar is covered with some 8 feet of water. Winds can affect water heights. Return earlier on windy days. If cut off the road will be passable in approximately 6 hours. Persons using the Bar Road do so at their own risk." A quotation such as "time and tide wait for no man" could have been quite appropriately added here.

A tour guide greets visitors and escorts them, convoy-style, across the seaweed- and shell-strewn, puddled path to

Minister's Island. Visitors usually cross with some trepidation (and perhaps a small prayer).

The tour includes the house, bathhouse, barn, and un-inhabited side of the island, where eighty protected deer and moose bound freely across the fields.

Sir William was the gentleman farmer of the island who raised imported Dutch belted black-and-white cattle and had extensive flower gardens and greenhouses with grapes and peaches. He had his produce and dairy products boxed and shipped by rail to his home in Montreal.

The unusual barn was designed by Van Horne himself, along with a young architect from Montreal named Edward Maxwell, who later designed many of the summer homes in St. Andrews. Story has it that Sir William built the windows high up so that his workers wouldn't be distracted by the outside.

Covenhoven may never be restored to the grandeur of 1901, with the perennial gardens, saltwater swimming pool, and windmill. But modern visitors can share one thing with Sir William Cornelius Van Horne: the extraordinary panorama of Passamaquoddy Bay.

In the Area

The Algonquin Hotel (St. Andrews): 506-529-8823

Atlantic Salmon Federation (Chamcook): 506-529-4581

Atlantic Salmon Information and Visitor Centre (Chamcook): 506-529-8889

Blue Peter Books (St. Andrews): 506-529-4466

Deer Island Point Camping Park (Lords Cove): 506-747-2423

Province of New Brunswick Department of Fisheries and Aquaculture, regional office (St. Andrews): 506-529-8930

Province of New Brunswick Heritage (Minister's Island):
506-529-3275

Province of New Brunswick—Provincial Parks (Campobello
Herring Cove): 506-752-2396

Province of New Brunswick Tourist Information Centre
(Campobello): 506-752-2997

Roosevelt Campobello International Park Commission
(Welshpool): 506-752-2922

St. Andrews Welcome Centre (Tourist Bureau): 506-529-3000

2 ~

Ferryland:

The Kingston Peninsula and Area

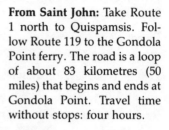

From Saint John: Take Route 1 north to Quispamsis. Follow Route 119 to the Gondola Point ferry. The road is a loop of about 83 kilometres (50 miles) that begins and ends at Gondola Point. Travel time without stops: four hours.

Highlights: *Gondola Point, ferries, Capt. William Abraham Pitt, the Kennebecasis River, spring freshets, covered bridge at Milkish Creek, Telegraph Hill, the St. John River, bird-watching, Woodman's Point, Long Reach, Victoria Beach, Browns Flat, Caton's Island, the oaks of Oak Point, Mistake Cove, steamboats, Belleisle Bay, Kingston, Trinity Church, Macdonald Consolidated School.*

What we'd like to do before setting out by car to explore the Kingston Peninsula would be to take a helicopter ride over it. With a clear overview, directions (which, summed up, sound something like "drive a few miles, take a ferry, drive a few miles, take another ferry, drive a few miles, etc.") wouldn't seem so bizarre. A visual image from a helicopter would be better, but here's a word picture of the Kingston Peninsula:

Imagine the mighty St. John River flowing from the top of New Brunswick down to the Bay of Fundy. As it nears the sea, it widens to the size of a lake. Imagine a finger-shaped island in the middle of this lake. Now, connect the top end of the island to the land, turning it into a peninsula. *Voilà*—we have the Kingston Peninsula.

The peninsula is a fascinating enigma. At the back doorstep of New Brunswick's largest and most industrialized city, it is pure and untouched. A short drive and a ferry ride away, it might as well be on the Miramichi. Every time we cross the water, we feel 50 kilometres farther and twenty years farther back in time.

Arriving at the Gondola Point wharf, we see our destination across the water—the spectacular green hills of the Kingston Peninsula. The houses that hug the steep banks of the Kennebecasis River have boats tied at their back steps and a million-dollar view. Lucky them.

There's a tiny park at the river's edge next to the ferry—it's a good place to swim or enjoy a sandwich. There are no public parks on the peninsula, so it's best to stop here. The boats come and go every twenty minutes or so, on demand, so there's no point in being in a hurry. While waiting for the ferry we have an opportunity to get our bearings. Clear water laps at the pebbled beach where we stand. The overlapping hills are a magnificent backdrop. The gaudily painted turquoise ferry, which looks like a mechanical bird with broken wings, seems very at home here.

The provincial tourist map is practically useless. The amount of detail needed is simply not there. (There are other maps that can be picked up at local tourist bureaus that are much better.) What we can get from a glance at the map is a general sense of where we will be going. Notice that the St. John River, flowing 450 miles from the northernmost parts of the province though Grand Falls, Woodstock, and Fredericton, is in the last stages of its journey down to the Bay of Fundy. The last segment of the river is called Long Reach. At Grand Bay it mixes with the waters of the Kennebecasis River and flows down to Saint John, where it roars through the Reversing Falls. Over half of New Brunswick's watershed drains through this narrow gorge into the salt water.

Parallel to Long Reach is the Kennebecasis, the beautiful river/lake that we are about to cross, equal in length and breadth to Long Reach, but fed by a much smaller stream.

The Kingston Peninsula, about 33 kilometres (20 miles) long and about 8 kilometres (5 miles) wide, is surrounded on three sides by the St. John River (Long Reach), the Kennebecasis River, and Grand Bay. There is almost as much water as land. Bridging it would be a gargantuan task. Instead land is connected to land by seven ferries, which are part of the New Brunswick highway system. The asphalt simply stops at the river's edge and the ferry takes over.

Used to rigidly scheduled, long crossing ferry rides, we were delighted with the "demand" system here. Barely missing the boat at one wharf, we could hardly believe it when the captain backed up to pick us up. Except during heavy traffic, the ferry will cross the whole river to pick up a single car.

As the boats are small, it is a good idea to avoid the times when residents are commuting to and from jobs in Saint John (6:00 to 8:00 A.M. and 4:00 to 6:00 P.M.). Fog can be an impediment, especially at night. On nights when a person can't see a hand in front of them (let alone a car on the other bank), frustrated residents drive the long land route around through Hampton.

The toll-free boat rides are a treat for tourists, Sunday drivers from Saint John, and residents, too, who love the isolated lifestyle on an *almost* island. Each boat has its own character. If the weather is fit, everyone gets out of their car to enjoy the sun on their face, or to scan the community bulletin boards. Advertised is everything from town hall meetings to furniture stripping services. In July and August there are maps to pick-your-own strawberries and blueberries. Lucky tourists find posters for traditional church suppers with ham, baked beans, and potato scallop, a home-cooked alternative to restaurant fare.

People have been ferried across this particular stretch of waves since the 1780s. Many passengers were farmers: women in bonnets and long skirts, men in homespun woolens. They journeyed across the river with their horses and wagons, tethered pigs and cows, ash splint baskets of apples and barrels of potatoes.

A plaque onboard honors Capt. William Abraham Pitt. Before the turn of the century he ferried people across the river in a simple scow equipped with a sail, long sculling oars, and a rudder. In choppy waters this was an unsteady and even dangerous means of transportation.

Captain Pitt had carried people from Reed's Point to Gondola Point and back for thirty years when he got a brilliant idea for a steadier, more reliable method for maneuvering a ship across the waves. His underwater-cable ferry was powered by a gasoline engine and pulled by means of a metal cable. Pitt built his homemade prototype out of things he had scrounged, including drums and rollers made out of tree trunks. He purchased the heavy steel cable and strung it across more than 1,500 metres (5,000 feet) of water by dragging it over the winter ice on a sled pulled by a team of horses.

The amazing new invention actually worked and since 1903 has served as the basic design for other cable ferries in New Brunswick and elsewhere.

Leaving the ferry, turn left on Route 845 west to Westfield (which is not on the peninsula, but that's what the sign says).

One of the most striking vistas of the whole journey comes up almost immediately. Beautiful birches and maples overhang the steep road gouged into the salmon-coloured bluff. These are the lush hardwoods we admired earlier from over a kilometre across the river. Unintimidated daisies grow up in cracks in the rock face. Over the guardrail, the shoulder drops off steeply to the river for an unimpeded view up North Channel where we can see the main river, the north side of Long Island, and smaller Mather Island at its tip.

Driving downstream, the river widens and there is a subtle change in the colour of the water from blue to brown. This part of the river is tidal, which means that when the tide is high on the shores of the Bay of Fundy at Saint John, the swell has a ripple effect. It raises the level of the river about half a metre (two feet) at Grand Bay but the water level diminishes to only a third of a metre (a foot) by the time it reaches the ends of Long Reach and Kennebecasis Bay.

More important than tides to people who live at the river's edge are the effects of the spring freshets, the engorged river created by rainfall and runoff from melting winter snow. In the spring, the river flow is high and fast. It calms down in June and is positively low by the end of the summer. The ferries have two ramp heights, one especially to accommodate the high level during the spring freshet season, the other for normal water levels.

After this exceptional river drive through humps and hillocks, the road goes inland for about 8 kilometres (5 miles). The area was once marginally farmed but now the only crop seems to be one of house lots. The adventurous who want to get down to the river can follow two rough side roads to the left: one to Moss Glen and another on the Nail Factory Road. There is a side road to White Head with a view of Long Island and the hills beyond.

At Summerville a ferry goes to Kennebecasis Island. Another, the *Romeo and Juliet*, takes passengers to Millidgeville (near the Saint John area) but does not run year-round.

We cross Milkish Creek at Bayswater through an old-fashioned covered bridge. *Milkish* is a Maliseet word meaning "place for drying fish," as this part of the river was a favourite fishing spot.

Although covered bridges were originally designed for their practicality—the roof protects the roadway and piers underneath—people like to tell stories. Some say that covered bridges were built to fool horses into thinking they were going home to the barn so they wouldn't be spooked by the torrential waters below. Others say that roofs were built to keep snow off the road. A contradictory tale says that in the old days men shovelled snow onto the bridge so that the runners of the horse-drawn sleds would glide more easily (which makes us wonder if they do this today for snowmobiles and cross-country skis). For those of us hardened by freeway driving, the pass through the sun-dappled wooden tunnel is all too brief.

Up on the right is a 150-metre (500-foot) rise known locally as Telegraph Hill. In 1794, commander in chief, His Royal Highness the Duke of Kent gave orders to establish a semaphore telegraph line from Halifax to Fredericton. The trees at the tops of designated hills were cut down and a communications system of signalling with flags from hill to hill was to be instituted. It is not known whether the system worked. As W. F. Ganong, a historian, commented in 1899, one would have to delve into British military records for the answer.

From here to the Harding's Point ferry the road runs through four miles of rugged inland hills. Following the ripples of the earth's surface, the road is a bit of a roller-coaster ride.

We catch the Harding's Point ferry where Long Reach (St. John River) makes a dramatic ninety-degree turn. From the middle of the river we see the trembling channel of Long Reach flowing downstream to join the Kennebecasis in swollen Grand Bay.

Off the ferry ramp we look back at the land across the water and see the rectangular southern end of the Kingston Peninsula.

Turn right on Route 177 toward Westfield. A sign in the window of the Westfield Country Store advertises a peculiar mixture of wares: fireworks, worms and crawlers, chips, and pop.

Continue on this road for 2.5 kilometres (1.5 miles), with Long Reach on the right. The lighthouse we see is at Belyeas Point. Turn right across a long arched bridge that crosses a large marsh at the mouth of the Nerepis River. As we turn right on Route 102 north, a sign tells us whether the Evandale ferry is running. It is considerate of the New Brunswick Department of Highways to point this out to us before we make plans to go farther upriver. We definitely want to catch that ferry!

Marshland is an important feeding and nesting ground for birds. In summer we saw dozens of red-winged blackbirds, who fasten their nests to the stems of cattails. In the spring (from late March to May), migrating aquatic birds such as Canada geese and a variety of ducks rest here on their way north.

Tourism New Brunswick publishes a free pamphlet called *Birdwatching New Brunswick Canada*, which we picked up at a tourist bureau. Folding like a map, it fits in our glove compartment. It includes such information as prime areas for birdwatching; advice for year-round birding; notes on Maritime nest records, as well as contact persons, organizations, and a bibliography.

Just over the bridge at Woodman's Point is a cairn dedicated to Sieur Charles de Boishebert and the fort that he occupied at this spot. It is easy to see why this point, sited with a clear view upstream and downstream, was an ideal spot for a fort. In 1749, de Boishebert made a valiant last effort to defend the French in Acadie. When it became apparent that the English would win the battle, he and his followers destroyed the fort and fled through the woods to an island in the Miramichi, which was later named after him. Unfortunately, remnants of the knoll where the fort stood were destroyed during the construction of the railway.

At Greenwich Hill turn right on Victoria Beach Wharf Road and follow this lovely country lane for 1.25 kilometres (.75 mile) to the beach. Gaudy devil's paintbrushes and purple vetch poke their way through the rocks. It's a great spot for collecting sand-polished driftwood and throwing stones. The river banks have everything from elegant twelve-hop skipping stones to soak-your-pants splashers.

Back to the corner, turning right on Route 102, we climb a ridge known as Devil's Back. The road heads inland here because the bluffs at the water's edge rise 120 metres (400 feet). No one settled this inhospitable ridge but the modern railway blasted a path through the rock next to the water. With the demise of the railway, this has now become a rough hiking trail. (It is a 1.6-kilometre, or 4-mile, walk from Victoria Beach to Browns Flat, where the railway path crosses Route 102.) Along Devil's Back, the elevation rises steadily, crowning at 443 metres (1,462 feet), 8 kilometres (5 miles) from the river at Mount Champlain (on the Kings and Queens County border).

Browns Flat, an intervale at the edge of the river, was a much more hospitable place to settle. In 1894 the Atlantic Wesleyan Church started a summer colony called Beulah Camp. With 200 cottages, it is still thriving today and has the feel of the old resort communities of past decades.

Caton's Island Road leads to the island that was one of the first places the French landed in New Brunswick. It was named after Captains Isaac and James Caton from Philadelphia, who were granted 2,000 acres in the 1760s and a license to trade with the Indians.

Much earlier, however, the island had been named "Ah-men-heik" by the Maliseet and later Isle au Garce and Eme-nenic by traders and fishermen from St. Malo. The first religious service on the St. John was held on this island in October 1611, led by Father Biard, a Jesuit missionary.

A mile past Browns Flat is a friendly diner called the Island View Canteen, a great place to stop for a cup of coffee in tourist season. Perched on a steep embankment, it looks down on Whelpley Cove, Caton's Island, and a bevy of sailboats. There's a yard sale every Saturday, and the Sunday specials are roast turkey and baked haddock and sauce.

Oak Point is a provincial park in which to camp for the night or relax for the day. It is a flat, sandy, pleasant spot on the banks of the St. John River. True to its name, hundreds of oaks grace this site. Some are over half a metre (two feet) wide at the base with branches angled to support perched children and adults. Others are so large and hollow that children can play inside them. Oak trees growing right on the sand beach have developed a means of surviving the spring freshets. They stand tall on their exposed roots, like mangroves.

Upstream is Mistake Cove, a 5-kilometre-long (3-mile-long) sock that can be easily confused with the main channel of the river. While a certain Captain Coy once made the simple mistake of sailing in here, his real mistake was probably in telling anyone about it. For years, river people continued to get a good laugh out of his misadventure, calling the spot Coy's Mistake. Today it is simply called Mistake Cove.

Next to the park is Saint Paul's Anglican Church at Greenwich. In the graveyard rest early Loyalist families: Flaglors, Flewellings, and Whelpleys. A walk around the cedar-shaded grounds gives us insight into country churches of 100 years ago, when they were the centre of people's lives.

Parishioners faithfully walked for miles, and rowed across choppy waters, every Sunday.

On to Evandale, where fresh vegetables, raspberries, and strawberries are sold at the roadside. Take Route 124 to Norton and the Evandale ferry. Near the ferry is the Eveleigh Hotel, billed as "the last of the riverboat hotels."

Crossing the St. John River at Evandale

Doris Calder, in her book *All Our Born Days: A Lively History of New Brunswick's Kingston Peninsula*, devotes a whole chapter to steamboats and hotels. Between 1816 and 1946 boats zigzagged from wharf to wharf along the river, collecting people and freight. Their ultimate destinations were Fredericton and Saint John.

The riverboats carried barrels of apples and live chickens from farmers on the Kingston Peninsula and returned with supplies from the city, such as flour and furniture. When the flags were flown at half-mast, everyone along the shore knew that a body was onboard.

One of the happy results of the paddle-wheel steamer was that it made the peninsula more accessible to city folk. Tourist hotels and boardinghouses mushroomed on the banks of the Kennebecasis and Long Reach. Eventually a more efficient railway and then automobile travel brought an end to the river hotel. The Eveleigh opened its doors to guests in 1890 and over 100 years later is still serving homemade gingerbread. Boaters tie up at the hotel dock.

We cross the river on the Evandale ferry. On the right the St. John meets Belleisle Bay. Near here, high up on a hill, in 1736, Sieur de Belle-Isle, grandson of Charles La Tour, built a habitation called "Nid d'Aigle"—Eagle's Nest. In 1755, when deportation of all Acadians was imminent, most of his family fled to Quebec, but their name remains.

Leaving the ferry, stay on Route 124 east to the Belleisle Shore Road and the Belleisle Bay ferry. On the other side, at Bate's Landing, turn right to Kingston on Route 850 and follow Belleisle Bay for 8.3 kilometres (5 miles).

This is serious cottage and marina country with boat rentals and restaurants—we feel jolted back into the twentieth century. Follow Kingston Creek, also known as Portage Creek, into the interior of the peninsula to Kingston. The

Maliseet, and later the Acadians and Loyalists, travelled this same route as a shortcut to the Kennebecasis and the sea.

Kingston is not a town but a crossroads with a high-spired church, a gas station, and a school. Designed to be the shiretown of Kings County, its remote location did not contribute to its growth, and eventually Hampton, a little farther upstream, got the population and the honors.

Trinity Anglican Church, constructed in 1789 by Loyalists from Connecticut and New York, is a National Historic Site. The old rectory, built in 1787, is still inhabited. Across the street is a small museum in the Macdonald Consolidated School, which also has an interesting history.

The original school, opened in 1905, was the first consolidated school in the province. Built largely with funds contributed by Sir William C. Macdonald, millionaire and founder of the Macdonald Tobacco Company, it was considered a model school. As an indication of how times have changed, it should be noted that the children were "bussed" to school in horse-drawn vans and that each child was required to tend a small garden plot on the school grounds.

From Kingston we wend our way back to the Kennebecasis on the road, which faithfully follows the historic portage of the Maliseet. There, the ferry takes us back to Gondola Point and the end of our journey.

In the Area

Beulah Camp Grounds (Browns Flat): 506-468-2286

Canadian Wildlife Service, Atlantic Region (bird-watching) (Sackville): 506-536-3025

The Eveleigh Riverboat Hotel (Evandale): 506-425-9993

Island View Canteen (Browns Flat): 506-468-2895

Kennebecasis Naturalist's Society (Box 12, Sussex, N.B.
    E0E 1P0)

Province of New Brunswick—ferries:

(Belleisle Bay): 506-485-2457

(Evandale): 506-485-2483

(Reed's Point/Gondola): 506-763-2370

(Westfield/Harding's Point): 506-763-2299

Province of New Brunswick—parks (Oak Point):
    506-468-2266

Trinity Anglican Church Rectory (Kingston): 506-763-2371

Westfield Country Store (Westfield): 506-757-2916

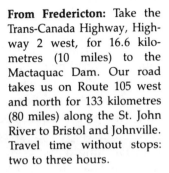

3 ~

River

Towns

of the

St. John

From Fredericton: Take the Trans-Canada Highway, Highway 2 west, for 16.6 kilometres (10 miles) to the Mactaquac Dam. Our road takes us on Route 105 west and north for 133 kilometres (80 miles) along the St. John River to Bristol and Johnville. Travel time without stops: two to three hours.

Highlights: *Mactaquac Dam, Mactaquac Fish Culture Station, Mactaquac Provincial Park, Nackawic Bend, ferries, Woodstock, Hartland, the world's longest covered bridge, Florenceville, potato fields, Johnville.*

As we leave Fredericton, our journey takes us on Route 105, the eastern "Sunday drive" side of the St. John River. We travel northerly and westerly, upriver, against the current.

As modern travellers we choose from a complex network of overland routes. But for earlier peoples, the aboriginals and settlers, the only break through the dense forests and inhospitable rocky ridges was on water. Rivers, lakes, and streams were as important to them as our modern highways are to us.

But the St. John River was more than a transportation system. It was a lifeline. It provided the basic necessities of life: drinking and wash water and food. The river teemed with beaver, muskrat, salmon, eels, and trout. Supplies, mail, and gossip were delivered by boat. The massive energy of the river was harnessed to drive logs and lumber down to Saint John and world markets. Flowing tributaries were bridled to turn gristmills and sawmills.

Scanning a New Brunswick map, it is easy to see that the St. John is an exceptional waterway. In earlier times the Maliseet paddled its full length by canoe. The French kept in touch with far-flung outposts by travelling (with a few portages) from Quebec City down to the river's mouth at Saint John and across to Port Royal in Nova Scotia. In the nineteenth century, during economic boom times, timber was driven from as far north as Madawaska down to the Bay of Fundy, making Saint John one of the most prosperous ports in British North America.

As modern road travellers we choose this route because of the placid beauty of the river. Except for a few pleasure craft, most of what we see on our drive will be clear, blue river water, uncomplicated by human adventure. One hundred and fifty years ago it was bustling with wharves and log booms, ferries and barges.

During the next 150 kilometres (90 miles), with the river as our companion, it will be difficult not to notice ghosts of river life past. The irony of this is that this modern river that we cherish looks more like the "goodly river" or "Oolahs-took" that the Maliseet knew than the river of the European settlers. Except that the banks of the goodly river, from Fredericton to Woodstock, are not the same as they once were. The favorite camping spots of the native peoples, the flat spots near the mouths of running brooks and river islands, were drowned when the floodgates of the Mactaquac Dam shut tight in 1967. Curiously, the dam is where our journey begins.

There is a dramatic lookoff above the hydroelectric facility with the blue hills of the Keswick Ridge behind. On the downstream side of the penstock is the St. John River, rushing off in its own fashion. Behind the dam is artificially swollen Mactaquac Lake, which was created when tiny Mactaquac Stream and the high-powered river were backed up by this mammoth concrete embankment.

We enjoy the sweeping view as we drive right across the top of the dam, past a grid of wires and robotlike creatures that support them. For a closer look at the Mactaquac generating station, New Brunswick Power offers tours from May through August.

Another attraction in the area is the Mactaquac Fish Culture Station. The construction of the dam put a virtual stop to the migrating salmon who annually return to the St. John from the sea to spawn in its headwaters. The Federal Department of Fisheries and Oceans built this station just below the dam to collect about 28,000 adult fish who congregate here every year. Five hundred are selected for broodstock and the rest are trucked upriver and released above other dams and natural obstacles such as Grand Falls.

Across the causeway is Mactaquac Provincial Park. After the lake (or headpond, as it is properly called) was created, the province took advantage of the waterfront property, setting 560 hectares (1,400 acres) aside for a park. The boundaries are marked with a traditional split-rail fence, which zigzags along the road. The main focus of the park is, naturally, the water, and visitors can enjoy two supervised beaches and separate sailboat and powerboat marinas as well as six well-maintained nature trails.

The campground is quite luxurious as campgrounds go, with kitchen shelters, heated bathrooms with hot showers, and sites with electrical hookups. This would be a good place to set up camp for a few days to explore the Fredericton area or to pick strawberries at a nearby farm. The civilized nature of the park and organized recreational activities such as paddleboats ($5.00 for thirty minutes), canoes ($6.00 per hour), and waterskiing make it a good place for children. It'll be hard to keep the children out of the water, but they must be eighteen to rent the boats. For adults, there is a lodge with a licensed dining room and an eighteen-hole golf course.

Leaving the park, turn left on Route 105. The view across the river is a patchwork of fields with a strip of woods at the crest. On a still day, the trees at the river's edge are joined at the base with their mirrored likenesses.

This lovely pastoral road is a mixture of farms and summer cottages, apple orchards and Herefords, stables and potato fields. A lone cyclist is a more common sight than a heavy truck. Those wanting to make time will be on the other side of the river on the speedy Trans-Canada. We cruise down Route 105 at a comfortable 80 kilometres per hour (about 50 miles per hour).

A glance at the map shows a distinct lack of place names along the river from Fredericton to Woodstock, as compared to, say, a similar 100-kilometre (60-mile) stretch from Woodstock to Perth-Andover.

Past Bear Island Cove a scenic bow appears upriver. Coming up is Nackawic Bend. From here the road rises high above the river, and we travel through an area with some sense of history and enjoy views of farmhouses with split-rail fences and giant sugar maples planted a century ago. Off in the distance, however, is a grey haze. If the wind is just right (or wrong), we are hit by an industrial stench coming from a pulp and paper mill and a chemical company.

Soon we cross a unique A-frame suspension bridge into the town of Nackawic—a nice, tidy little community. Everything looks bright and new, because it is . . . only twenty-five years old.

Two thousand people were displaced by the creation of the Mactaquac headpond in the late 1960s. Forced to leave homesteads where their families had been rooted for five generations, they moved their houses, barns, churches, and even their dead, for they even dug up and moved their graveyards.

Everything in the way of the rising river was moved or destroyed. Residents watched as the Hawkshaw Bridge was blown up by the army. The river's edges were shaved of ancient trees and shrubs and burnt in a pyre, along with any nonmovable buildings.

The instant town was built on expropriated farmland, surveyed into neat little lots, designed for flooded-out families and newly arrived mill workers. There are no obvious signs of the human tragedy involved in its creation. Time seems to have healed the wounds.

Looking back with a modern, environmentally sensitive perspective, it seems almost impossible to believe that a similar evacuation and inundation could take place here today.

The modern town offers amenities to the traveller, including a small shopping centre. The riverside park at Nackawic features a beautiful view of the bend where we look back down the river from whence we have just come.

Follow Otis Drive back to the main road, Route 105. The river narrows substantially 5 kilometres or so (a few miles) down the road at Southampton. Pokiok Stream on the west side of the river was the site of a red granite gorge with a 21-metre (70-foot) roaring waterfall until the flooding swallowed it up.

Before the days of bridges, the river was not as large a barrier as it might have been to community life. There were ferries, usually only big enough to carry a horse and buggy, that crossed back and forth across the river. Families from Culliton and Southampton were related to families in Pokiok and Hawkshaw.

In summer towboats transported passengers and goods. These flat-bottomed scows, called freight or store boats, were pulled by horses with special harnesses and with ropes attached to the masts of the boats. They labored along special "tow paths" next to the river. On the return trip, downstream, the horse and driver would board the boat and ride home with the flow.

In winter, the river froze into a solid road. People drove horses and sleighs on the road of ice many miles upstream to Woodstock or downstream to Fredericton for provisions.

Past Southhampton the river narrows between intimate gravel cliffs. We can no longer see the Trans-Canada on the other side because it has ventured inland. Instead we see pretty birch copses and not much evidence of human life. This is what the river must have felt like 300 years ago.

Leaving Upper Southhampton, we are greeted by masses of black-eyed Susans along the side of the road. Another time of year, it might be daisies and red clover, or Queen Anne's lace and purple asters.

The stretch near Meductic where the Trans-Canada crosses the Eel River was once considered one of the five most beautiful views in Canada. Now it is a strange sight: half of the top of the hill has been clear-cut of trees while the other half is still wooded.

Meductic (based on the Maliseet word *medoctec*, meaning "the end") was a permanent camp of the Maliseet. In the mid 1800s the Maliseet people were removed to a purchased site 3 kilometres (2 miles) below Woodstock (now called Woodstock Indian Reserve 23).

A horse team in the apple orchard

Coming up on the right is a large Greek Revival farm-house with three connected barns. This is a taste of the exceptional architecture that awaits us in Woodstock.

In an apple orchard nearby the trees have ancient and gnarled limbs. In the fall we sometimes see apples for sale in baskets at the roadside. What we are looking for are apples we can't get in the supermarket—the historic varieties.

At the turn of the century hundreds of varieties of apples were grown, each with a documented shape (round to conical),

35

color (red, green, yellow, with variations of blush), and especially flavor (spicy, sharp, sweet, and tart). Because these varieties were not commercially viable on a large scale, they are now usually found growing in old, out-of-the-way orchards.

Frances Peabody Sharp, a local Woodstock resident, is famous in apple circles for developing, through methodical hybridizing, several varieties, including the New Brunswicker, Walden, Munro Sweet, and Crimson Beauty.

Woodstock is up and across the river. We are glad to be on the slow side of the river. The grass and pineapple weed grow right up to the asphalt—no fancy shoulders and passing lanes here. But soon we will be crossing over. At Woodstock the Trans-Canada cuts away from the river's edge, giving us the choice of two river roads.

At junction 585 turn left and cross the bridge to Woodstock. This river approach to Woodstock is infinitely more interesting than the highway approach. Most people who have sped by on their way from southern New Brunswick to Quebec, or who have crossed the American border at Houlton, think of Woodstock as a highway strip of gas stations and motels. On their way into Woodstock from the highway they are greeted by suburbia, a campground, and a racetrack.

But the heart and soul of Woodstock is the river bank. Most old homes in Woodstock face the river. Downtown Main Street parallels the river. The red-bricked downtown was constructed around 1880 after a terrible fire had razed many of the wood-framed buildings. This fireproof brick block was considered a model of "modern" town planning because of its uniform building design.

The town straddles two sides of an intervale called the Gully at the mouth of the Meduxnekeag River. This makes getting around town a bit of a challenge. It's best not to try doubling back more than a few blocks from the river. Too many roads lead back to the Trans-Canada.

There is a friendly tourist bureau on King Street next to the farmers' market on the waterfront. They give out street maps and advice.

Like many small towns in the Maritimes, Woodstock is struggling economically, but the downtown has a surprising diversity of shops: a bookstore, china shop, bakery, library, and restaurants. This is a good place to stop for lunch.

The L. P. Fisher Library at 679 Main Street has on display two cases of Maliseet stone artifacts: arrowheads, spearheads, knives, hide scrapers. This is part of the extensive collection of a native son, noted author, historian, and amateur archaeologist Dr. G. F. Clarke. (In his book *Someone Before Us* he bemoans the fact that the creation of the Mactaquac headpond will submerge, forever, dozens of ancient Native American campsites.)

The town is a treasure for students of architecture. Within an area of ten square blocks, off Main Street, are thirty-two historic residential and commercial buildings built in the second half of the nineteenth century. Architectural styles represented include Greek Revival, Gothic Revival, Queen Anne Revival, Beaux Arts school, Second Empire, Foursquare architectural style, Italianate Romanesque Revival, and neo-classical. A pamphlet called *Woodstock Walkabout* identifies and describes them in detail.

The Owl Place Bookstore sells a beautifully illustrated book by Allison Connell called *A View of Woodstock*. The author has included photographs and etchings of homes as they looked in their prime, complete with wrought-iron fences and some fascinating interior shots of Victorian domestic life.

Leaving Woodstock, we stay on the west side of the river, on Route 103, heading toward Hartland. We look forward to plunging into potato country.

The landscape is a gentle panorama. The fields have been cleared from the river to the tops of the hills. Then the road

37

veers away from the river. When we do return, we get a glimpse of the famous bridge—the longest covered bridge in the world. Soon we leave Route 103, turning right toward the bridge, Hartland, and Route 105.

There's a shaded rest area (with pit toilet, water fountain, and picnic tables) on the steep banks of the river at the foot of the bridge. A lookoff gives us a chance to peruse this unusual structure. There are plaques describing the history of the bridge, which was declared a historic site in 1980.

Bridges of this type were covered mainly to preserve their wooden trusses. The original bridge dates back to the turn of the century, when a three-cent toll was charged for pedestrians and a twelve-cent toll for a double team of horses and wagon.

Back then the decision to cover the bridge was a controversial one. Upstanding citizens felt that rough characters might congregate in it at night, scaring women and children. For years a sign warned against driving faster than a walk across the bridge. The penalty was $20.00. Apparently the sound of horses galloping through the wooden structure with a wagon in tow was enough to wake the dead. The vibrating hooves and wheels also created an unhealthy sway to the structure.

It's necessary, as when driving through a tunnel, to flick on headlights before entering the bridge, which is about half a kilometre (or one-quarter of a mile) long. The bridge can also be crossed by pedestrians; a covered sidewalk, added in 1947, is a kind of mini covered bridge strapped to the side.

The cozy bridge is supposed to be a good place to kiss (especially in a buggy) or make a wish (while holding one's breath for the entire span). We were sure to take advantage of these opportunities.

Just off the ramp of the bridge is the Hartland tourist bureau, where 20,000 people signed the guest book last year. It's a good guess that the world's longest covered bridge is the drawing card. The area is also known to hunters. The tourist bureau directs nonresident (bear, deer, grouse, and woodcock) hunters to local outfitters who offer package deals including rooms, meals, a guide, and a license.

Hartland is a pretty brick streetscape paralleling the river; a tiny village of 900 people that boasts that it is "the smallest incorporated town in Canada."

Every July Hartland hosts its "Spud and Spoke Days," which features tractor-trailer competitions and old favourites such as the draft horse show and the "potato barrel rolling contest." The event is open to all comers. Enthusiastic visitors please note: rolling those wooden barrels is a tricky business. They are brimming with potatoes—and there are no covers.

A few miles north of Hartland the Trans-Canada (Highway 2) crosses over to the east side of the river. Travellers in a hurry to head back to Fredericton or up toward Edmundston can connect with the big road here.

The big highway spans the St. John on a six-half-moon bridge. Cars and trucks zip over us as we continue our leisurely journey on Route 105.

Here the river takes on a different personality: lots of little ponds and pools that, no doubt, make salmon very happy. Becaguimec, which translates as "place where the salmon lie," is the name of a stream and island here. The river is easygoing and lazy, and the low-sloping hills have a relaxed feeling, too.

Florenceville is the corporate headquarters of McCain's Foods, Ltd., a food-processing conglomerate. The family business started here, in Florenceville, in 1957, producing frozen french fries. The McCain brothers understood increasing consumer desire for more convenience and processed foods and expanded into frozen vegetables, pizza, and juices. Today they have annual sales of $3 billion, with 12,500 employees and 40 factories worldwide. Unfortunately there are no tours, but the Andrew and Laura McCain Library and Art Gallery is open to the public.

We continue up to Bristol, a sleepy little town with comfortable old houses and stores fronting the river. Three railways cars parked on an abandoned spur line belong to the Shogomoc Historical and Model Railway Club. They are restoring these remnants of the once thriving rail line that served this area for more than a century.

The scenic town of Bath is the end of our journey, except for one last diversion into the back country, turning right on Route 565 and heading to Johnville.

We hit gravel and the ambrosia of fresh clover. Potato fields spread out on both sides of us like green corduroy. The river in its valley trough drops below us as we climb into the hills. The view, spanning fields and woods, to the far-off mountain ridges is exhilarating.

For the last few hours we have been riding a narrow shelf focused in on the river. We had almost forgotten that a vista such as this was possible: ten mountains, superimposed one over the other. It's just a quarter of a turn to an equally impressive scene: hills dipping down into a valley; at the centre, a clear blue lake.

The Johnville area (including Kilfoil, Murphy's Corner, and Killoween) was settled (you guessed it) by Irish people and the community is centered around Saint John the Evangelist Roman Catholic Parish. A cairn next to the church is dedicated to the memory of the Rt. Rev. John Sweeney, Bishop of Saint John, who founded the settlement in 1861.

Every year since the 1860s, a picnic has been held on the church grounds the first Wednesday of August. Families have attended for generations. Fortunate visitors are also welcome to participate in the fun of the community meal. They say that there is dancing under the stars.

After the breathtaking view from what seems like the top of the world, it is time to loop our way back down to the St. John River valley. Past the church, the road angles to the right through lovely fields, some abandoned. Into the trees and out into the extraordinary vista again, and we descend. Turn right at the yield sign back onto the pavement, to a stop sign, and turn left to Bath.

In the Area

Andrew and Laura McCain Library and Art Gallery (Florenceville): 506-392-5294

Hartland Tourist Centre: 506-375-4075

L. P. Fisher Library (York Regional) (Woodstock): 506-328-6880

Mactaquac Dam (Mactaquac): 506-363-3093

Mactaquac Fish Culture Station (Mactaquac): 506-363-3021

Nackawic Tourist Information: 506-575-2037

The Owl Book Place, Ltd. (Woodstock): 506-328-8970

Province of New Brunswick—parks (Mactaquac): 506-363-3011

Woodstock Chamber of Commerce Tourist Information Centre: 506-325-9049

4 ~

The Acadian Peninsula:

Caraquet to Miscou

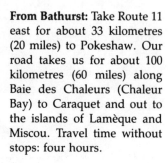

From Bathurst: Take Route 11 east for about 33 kilometres (20 miles) to Pokeshaw. Our road takes us for about 100 kilometres (60 miles) along Baie des Chaleurs (Chaleur Bay) to Caraquet and out to the islands of Lamèque and Miscou. Travel time without stops: four hours.

Highlights: *Pokeshaw Provincial Park, Grande-Anse Tourist Bureau, Popes' Museum, Acadian Historical Village, Caraquet, Carrefour de la Mer, Acadian Festival, Shippagan, Aquarium Marine Centre, Lamèque, Baroque Music Festival, Miscou.*

Our journey into the heart of Acadia starts simply enough at a picnic park. Pull into Pokeshaw Provincial Park, and look out at the magnificent Baie des Chaleurs. The land is surprisingly flat but the drop-off is dramatic. Clearly all the drama here belongs to the sea.

The land was cleared at some point, but the fields of this windswept coast are not quite farms. Probably as soon as a farmer was offered any other option to support his family, he jumped at the chance.

Just offshore is a sea stack, an island high up out of the aggressive waves. A few decades ago we would have been able to walk out to the edge of the peninsula and gasp at the crashing surf below. Now it is separated from the mainland, an island rookery. It is a veritable paradise for double-crested cormorants who nest noisily, cheek by jowl with their friends, from May until September. Their messy habits make us grateful for the safe olfactory distance between us. Cormorants leave dead fish parts all over the place and build seaweed nests in trees, which eventually die from bird excreta.

It would be easy to fritter away a whole afternoon watching these birds. They swim with their bodies submerged with only their heads and necks visible. When they go after a fish they can plunge down to a depth of 7 metres (25 feet). Their feathers are only partially waterproof, so they bask with outspread wings in the sun, like so many soggy umbrellas.

Sailing in here during a heat wave in July of 1534, Jacques Cartier named this body of water Baie des Chaleurs, or "Warm Bay." The mountainous land mass seen about 23 kilometres (14 miles) across the water is Quebec's Gaspé Peninsula, where Cartier planted a 9-metre (30-foot) cross.

The wave motion here is interesting. Cold, fresh surface water from the Gaspé current enters on the north side of the bay and travels into the bay, where it has nowhere else to go but back out. It travels along the south coast (where we stand), creating a counterclockwise gyre of surface water. This guarantees bathers an even 24°C (72°F) water temperature at beaches peppered along the shore. A fence protects us from the sudden drop over the edge of the sandstone cliffs, but there is a steep path down to the beach below.

Pokeshaw is not only for bird-watching. The Pokeshaw River runs across the variegated pebbles and into the beer-coloured water, making for a lovely spot to spend the day, if you're feeling lazy.

The picnic park itself is tiny (about half a dozen tables) but very busy. People bring their binoculars to study the birds, and a picnic, often cooked lobster, which they crack

43

open and relish in the fresh air. There is an old-fashioned hand pump, which is very popular with the children. They crowd around it, learning the knack of priming, before the final gush overflows into cupped hands.

Many of the license plates are from Quebec and Ontario, and based on snippets of conversation we overhear, the travellers are mostly Francophones. This corner of the province may be one of the best-kept secrets of French-speaking tourists.

Turn left out of the park and just ahead is a sign that reads, "Village Historique Acadien 16 km."

A few miles down the road is Grande-Anse, where a lighthouse-shaped tourist information bureau sits next to a larger-than-life lobster trap. There is a picnic table inside the trap and traveling children can't resist it.

The student staff is friendly and bilingual, so we try out our high-school French. (They are very understanding.) They tell us where to find the best beaches on this coast. It pays to ask because the beaches are not necessarily visible from the road.

Grande-Anse is the first of many fine beaches from which to choose. It has caves and pillars gouged out of eroded sandstone cliffs. Other beaches are at Plage Anse-Bleue and Maisonnette. Boats can be rented for a look at more remote coastline.

Tourist pamphlets are printed mostly in the French language, so we ask many questions of the bilingual staff. On a hot summer day, it is very important to remember that *crème glacée* is ice cream.

One of the major destinations of this area, especially for members of the Roman Catholic faith, is the Musée des Papes or Popes' Museum. The museum offers a retrospective of the history of the papacy, a large collection of liturgical articles and exhibits relating to the religious dimension of Acadian heritage. The main exhibit is an exact scale model of St. Peter's Basilica. Every detail has been reproduced, including 330 statues around the square and real water gushing out of the fountains onto the flagstone pavement. The museum serves light meals in the dining room and also has outside picnic tables with a beautiful view of the bay.

After a beach diversion, follow Route 11 as it crosses the Rivière Nord (North River). On the right are piles of hay that have been stacked on cribwork above the marsh. They are called *chafauds*. Welcome to Village Historique Acadien (the Acadian Historical Village).

It's obvious that the creation of this village took a tremendous amount of imagination and effort. From all over the province the remnants of Acadian buildings were gathered together and trucked to this remote corner of the province. The 1875 printing shop came from Shediac, site of the weekly newspaper the *Moniteur Acadien*. The shoemaker's shop was transported from Neguac, the school from Chockpish. The homes came from places like Maisonnette, Inkerman, Memramcook, and Mazerolle Settlement. Many of the restored buildings originated in the Caraquet area, but the site of the actual village was a fresh, uninhabited field.

Walk into one of the cozy homes and inhale the fragrance of bread fresh out of the clay beehive oven. The mistress of the house sits in a rocking chair, in a long skirt, cap, and apron, with knitting in her lap. She tells us about the families whose presence still resonates within the wooden walls: the Babineaus, Legeres, Theriaults, and Godins.

The Acadians were French settlers who struggled for a century and a half to make homes for themselves in the New World. Unfortunately they became pawns in the battle between France and England. In 1755, the year of the tragic expulsion, 6,000 New Brunswick Acadians were shipped away. Some were sent to France but most were scattered down the

Eastern Seaboard as far south as Louisiana. Six thousand more fled north or into the woods.

The Acadians who managed to survive and return in spite of great adversity were not given back their former lush farmlands along the Annapolis and St. John Rivers. They were granted poor, remote coastal land that the Loyalists had rejected. To survive, the farmers became fishermen.

A fishing magnate from the Isle of Jersey named Jacques Robin took advantage of the Acadian plight by employing many men in the fishing industry, at near starvation wages. His company continued its economic stranglehold on the fishermen's lives for 100 years, until the twentieth century and the emergence of fishermen's cooperatives (*caisse populaire*). A "Robin Shed" from Caraquet, circa 1855, sits side by side with other buildings at the museum.

Neither Frenchmen nor Englishmen, the Acadians clung to their language and customs, which were centered around their church. The turning point was 1881, the year of the first Acadian convention at Memramcook. Delegates decided to retain their own identity separate from French-speaking Quebec. Symbolically, they chose a holiday, the Feast of the Assumption on August 15. Later they selected an Acadian flag consisting of the blue, red, and white flag of France with a golden star, and an Acadian hymn, "Ave Maris Stella," sung in Latin.

From that point on the Acadian culture came into its own. Acadians struggled for, and achieved, publicly funded education for their children in their own language and a French-speaking university in Moncton. New Brunswick presently has an officially bilingual legislature, court system, and public service.

It would be difficult to spend less than a few hours at the historic village. The buildings are spread out and only a few visitors are lucky enough to hitch a ride in the horse-drawn wagon. Like the Acadians, visitors travel the dusty roads

The Acadian Village

(avoiding the horse droppings) on foot. One of the perks of staying over the lunch hour is the authentic *poutine rapée* and *fricot* served in the cafeteria.

Like other "living" historical re-creations, the Acadian Village offers visitors an "immediate" sense of history that cannot be experienced by reading a book or watching a film about an era. Here we see the plain facts: the tragic history and the grueling life. But there is another dimension to this museum. The process of collecting and reconstructing the physical evidence of past lives helped this people, who are a very distinct and vibrant living culture, find a part of themselves that had been lost.

Acadia is not a place. It is a people who are spread throughout the Maritimes, Quebec, and the United States. Thousands of them visit this village every year.

Leaving the village, turn right on Route 11 and head toward Caraquet. The road travels along the edge of Caraquet Harbour to the town. Maisonnette is across the water and there is a glimmer of the Gaspé on the horizon.

Caraquet bustles by comparison to the shore we just travelled. There are stores and restaurants, live theatre and music. In the tourist season the nerve centre for travellers in Caraquet is Carrefour de la Mer, an upscale complex with a tourist bureau, restaurant, souvenir shop, and auditorium, smack in the middle of town on the wharf near a major fishing fleet.

The tourist bureau is very obliging. There's almost nothing they can't do for us. Want to tour a large fishing boat? Listen to a lecture on the development of the fishermen's union? Boat across to a small island to dig clams? Jig for cod? Fine, they'll make the arrangements.

Some tourists choose a tour of École des Pêches (New Brunswick School of Fisheries) or the Musée Acadien (Acadian Museum), which are both within walking distance of Carrefour de la Mer.

The fisheries school offers courses in everything from high-tech satellite-guided navigation to marine emergency methods, from marine engineering to net repairing. Through an international outreach program, students from Francophone countries in Africa and Central America come here to Caraquet to acquire knowledge and skills, which they take back to their home countries.

The Acadian Museum has interesting exhibits about Acadian life right up to modern times. A recent display chronicled the struggle for equality in education from 1850 to the present.

An exciting time to visit Caraquet would be during the Acadian Festival, which coincides with the Feast of the Assumption on August 15. The Gala de la Chanson features new singing talent and there's a colorful and very noisy celebration called *tintamarre* (which literally means "racket"). Everyone dresses up in costumes and takes to the street to make as much noise as possible—with bells, instruments, whistles, and even pot lids with wooden spoons.

Another celebration in the area is Festival Marin du Nouveau-Brunswick, held every July in Bas-Caraquet.

From Caraquet head south on Route 11 toward Shippagan and the islands of Lamèque and Miscou.

We leave behind the dramatic cliffs of Chaleur Bay. This is flat terrain that slopes gently to the sea. There is a serene beauty to this land, but it clearly has not had much to offer human beings who want to live off it. Still it is home to many.

The vegetation is very scrubby in places and will appeal to people with an eye for the remote. Like many coastal areas, the roads are not built for sightseers and do not follow the scenic coast as closely as we might like.

Our route, which starts at the turnoff near Pokemouche and continues to the tip of the peninsula at Shippagan across to the island of Lamèque and over to Miscou Island, is a

50-kilometre (30-mile) dead end. Those pressed for time may want to explore only part of the way.

Follow Route 11 to the turnoff at exit 217 to Shippagan. Through Inkerman follow the signs to Shippagan. Travelling up a flat peninsula, water and salt marsh appear on both sides of the road. The big brown fields are peat bogs. This is a major industry here and in Lamèque.

At the crossroads we have a choice: turn left to the provincial park to set up a camp, picnic, or swim, or turn right to the town.

Shippagan, a bustling fishing port (when the season and fish stocks allow), is called "New Brunswick's Commercial Fishing Capital." The wharf area is a congestion of blue and turquoise, wires and masts, long-liners and draggers, crab and lobster pots.

A good time to get caught up in the excitement of the fishing fleet is during the Provincial Fisheries Festival in July. The harbour is clogged with boats decorated to the hilt with thousands of coloured flags. During the Blessing of the Fishing Vessels they take lucky passengers for a steam out into the harbour.

One of the main tourist attractions in Shippagan is the Aquarium Marine Centre, which is devoted not to exotic imported species but to the sea life of the ocean within our view. There are tanks and tanks of fish and lobsters, sea anemones, and starfish, right out of the Gulf of St. Lawrence. Stare down a hideously ugly Atlantic hemitripterus or watch harbour seals frolic in the outside tank. They happen to be most entertaining at feeding times, so look for them between 11:00 A.M. and 4:00 P.M.

Cross from Shippagan to the island of Lamèque over a drawbridge and causeway. Local folks in a hurry are not pleased by the delay, but children think that the bridge swinging open to let a ship through is the next best thing to the seals at the aquarium.

Scanning the wide expanse of harbour, including a dozen wharves and a community of boats, stretching all the way out to the lighthouse, gives us some sense of how important the fishing industry is to the livelihood of the people here.

Welcome to Lamèque, famous for peat moss and baroque music, a strange but true combination. The island is not a beautiful place for touring but is fascinating nonetheless. Fairly industrialized, Lamèque hosts a major plant for horticultural peat as well as wharves and boats that mirror those we have just seen in Shippagan.

Almost simultaneously, in July, this island celebrates Festival Provincial de la Tourbe (Peat Moss Festival) and Festival International de Musique Baroque (Baroque Music Festival).

Peat moss is composed of layers and layers of sphagnum moss that has decayed under oxygen-deficient conditions. One generation of plants grows upon another and seals the layers below. It has great water-absorption qualities, which is why people add it to their gardens. The quality also creates the biggest challenge to harvesting it, as 95 percent of peat is water. This problem is solved with a crisscross of drainage ditches. For a guided tour of the peat operations, inquire in town.

The Baroque Music Festival has been inspired and directed since 1975 by Lamèque native Mathieu Duguay. He left his island home many years ago to study the harpsichord and developed a passion for music of the seventeenth century. What had humble beginnings has evolved into an annual world-class event.

Performances of the one-week-long festival take place in the Church of Sainte-Cecile in Petite-Rivière-de-l'Ile. The all-wooden church features fantastic acoustics and the church pews seat 320.

Last year the concert included the works of Vivaldi, del, Holborne, and Gibbons and such eighteenth-cer composers as Bach, Telemann, and Kuhnel. The perfor came from Germany, Italy, England, and Canada. The re Canada enjoyed the concerts, as well, on CBC radio.

The end of the road is Miscou Island, the island past island at the end of the peninsula. Until recently access only by ferry, now a bridge spans the waves.

Ironically, from a sea point of view, Miscou was not end of the line, but the first place to be spotted by Jacq Cartier in 1534. He named it Cap d'Esperance and a Europeans settled in. But it was never meant to suppo large population. The Mi'kmaq knew better. "Miscou" is derived from a Mi'kmaq word that means "boggy, low land."

As twentieth-century travellers we are glad that it has never been vastly popular. Acres upon acres of sand have collected along the shoreline, making Miscou one of the most serenely beautiful and peaceful places one could ask for.

In the Area

Acadian Historical Village (Caraquet): 506-727-3467

Acadian Museum (Caraquet): 506-727-3269

Aquarium Marine Centre (Shippagan): 506-336-4771

Caraquet Tourist Bureau: 506-727-6234

Carrefour de la Mer (Caraquet): 506-727-3637

Festival information, including Acadian Festival (Caraquet), Sea Festival (Bas-Caraquet), Provincial Fishery Festival (Shippagan), and Peat Moss Festival (Lamèque), call the Acadian Peninsula Tourist Association (Caraquet): 506-727-6622

International Baroque Music Festival (Lamèque): 506-344-5846

Lamèque Tourist Information Bureau: 506-344-8293

Popes' Museum (Grande-Anse): 506-732-3003

Province of New Brunswick—parks (Shippagan):
506-336-8673

Province of New Brunswick—School of Fisheries
(Caraquet): 506-727-6531

Theatre Populaire d'Acadie (Caraquet): 506-727-3403

PRINCE EDWARD ISLAND

5 ~
Souris
to the
East Point
Lighthouse

From the Wood Islands ferry: Take Route 315 north to Montague and Route 4 north to Dingwell's Mills and Route 2 east to Souris.

From Charlottetown: Take Route 2 east to Souris. The 33 kilometre (20-mile) road starts in Souris and follows the Northumberland Strait north to East Point, looping around to Elmira. Travel time without stops: forty-five minutes.

Highlights: *The ferry, Souris, Souris East Lighthouse, beaches, Red Point Provincial Park, Basin Head Fisheries Museum, East Point Lighthouse, North Lake, Elmira Train Museum.*

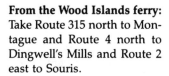

There is a common denominator for every person who comes to Prince Edward Island—everyone from the elderly fifth-generation Islander returning from a trip to Toronto to the two-month-old baby tourist arrives by boat.

Approaching on a mainland superhighway, perhaps speeding to make the ferry in that last tense hour, we queue up the car in the carefully delineated lines on the asphalt and heave a huge sigh of relief. There are no advance reservations, and we are pleasantly surprised to discover that the trip across is free. Visitors pay to get off the island.

The next hour is a lesson in patience. We wait our turn and do as we are told: drive up the ramp, inch the car along to comply with the frantic hand signals of the ferry employee, get out of car, and go up on deck.

The ferry steams out of port and into the waves of Northumberland Strait. An experienced Islander has the patience of Job and is prepared with a lunch and a crossword puzzle. The rest of us while away the next forty-five minutes (from New Brunswick) or hour and a half (from Nova Scotia) with various activities. In fine weather people congregate at the prow, which has the most spectacular view. Others hang over the railing, mesmerized by the plowing action of the boat against the choppy seas. In dicey weather the adventurous huddle on the outside decks, but on the sides, out of the wind. Most people enjoy the sea from inside the cozy cabin and catch a cafeteria coffee and a bite to eat.

By the time the boat docks and the loudspeaker rudely summons us to our cars, it doesn't matter whether the voyage has taken forty-five minutes or forty-five years. We arrive as if through a time warp, decidedly more relaxed after we are greeted by the red soils, fluorescent greens, and wide open blue sky of Prince Edward Island.

The first stop for most is the tourist information bureau. It is strategically placed, just off the ferry ramp. Map in hand, we try to get a sense of where things are and where we want to go.

One big question to ask bureau staff is how long it takes to get places. Some mental gears must be changed here because the scale of the map is 1:277,000, or 1 inch = 4 miles. The standard scale in New Brunswick and Nova Scotia is 1:640,000, or 1 inch = 10 miles. What this means is that we can drive from tip to toe of the island in three hours. If we don't like one place, we can be somewhere completely different in

The Northumberland ferry to Prince Edward Island

twenty minutes. Travellers can feel a strange sense of accomplishment in (seemingly) covering so much ground so fast.

Studying the map, we also notice a grid of roads that are very rarely more than 5 kilometres (3 miles) apart. The staff at the bureau reassure us that no one gets lost on this island with virtually no wilderness. It is recommended that confused off-islanders simply drive a kilometre or so to the next sign to pinpoint their whereabouts. (One kind farmer driving a tractor helped us out, too.)

The signage laws in this province are exceptional. Tacky and ugly is forbidden at roadside. Rather than a moving, flashing, neon chicken marking the spot, a simply lettered black sign reads "Joe's Chicken Emporium."

Geographic places are identified with green signs. And it's a good thing that they are. Outside the cities of Charlottetown and Summerside, P.E.I. has a remarkably lovely, homogenous landscape. The hills, potato fields, brooks, and cows on main Route 2 through Queens County are not that dissimilar from hills, potato fields, brooks, and cows on the back roads of eastern Kings County. After driving for hours, a visitor gains an almost holographic insight into the land, where the parts are the same as the whole. On a small island with a relatively consistent topography it is good that there are lots of signs.

There is no great advantage in covering a great deal of territory in a short time. The scale is small, and to appreciate island life is to appreciate minutiae: sunny yellow marsh marigolds thriving in puddles beside clay roads in the month of June or quartz crystals in a handful of apricot-colored sand dune. Standard advice to tourists that they get out of the car and smell the flowers is essential on P.E.I. In a tiny place, a precious view framed along thirty metres of road bank will dissolve into a green blur in the brief eye-blink of a speeding car.

The objective of our first tour in P.E.I. is to get off the beaten track, away from the 700,000 other tourists who visit the island every year. (Curiously, the resident population is only 130,000.) We head toward the top right tip of the island, eastern Kings County. There are no theme parks or fast-food restaurants here but the area is far from wild. The landscape, like the rest of P.E.I., has been tamed into gentle rolling farmland. The sea is another story.

Our drive begins in Souris, a small town of 1,500 people, the fifth largest community on P.E.I. As the commercial hub of the area, this is the place to pick up provisions and find a restaurant meal or a place to stay. There won't be any more shopping along this coast.

Driving over the crest and down into the town, there is a sweeping view to the left of the calm, estuarine Souris River, and to the right, the choppier waters of Colville Bay. The imposing Gothic red sandstone St. Mary's Catholic Church dominates the high ground.

The Souris East Lighthouse was the last staffed lighthouse on P.E.I. until it, too, was automated in 1991, and it is open to the public in the summer. Built in 1880, it served to keep ships safe in a range of eighteen nautical miles. The old equipment is still intact. Studying the ropes and pulleys and weights, one can imagine the strenuous efforts of the keeper of that light, whose job it was to ensure that a beacon shone out into the dark sea night.

Connecting East and West Souris are a bridge and a sand spit on which the provincial government has created a park. It is for day use only and is a good place to have a picnic and to enjoy the view. They say that swimming is best here at high tide when a person doesn't have to chase the water out too far. Before the construction of the bridge, this open river mouth was considered a safe haven and was full of ships.

Souris is the French word for "mouse." According to *Ten Farms Become a Town: A History of Souris, P.E.I., 1700-1920*, which can be purchased at the town hall, the name goes back to the 1700s. French sailors entering the bay were forced to cut through waves of drowned mice that had infested the land and swarmed right to the waters and into the drink.

This book is based on the papers of George Leard, a Souris citizen who had taken an interest in local history long before it was fashionable to do so. In his research he interviewed elderly people, collected newspaper clippings, maps, genealogies, and numerous other documents. His papers can be found on eighteen reels of microfilm in the Public Archives in Charlottetown.

The photographs in *Ten Farms* give readers a poignant insight into the evolution of this community. There are streetscapes with wooden sidewalks and hitching posts; and the harbour is a forest of sailboat masts. It is difficult not to feel a touch of nostalgia for the past.

One street of early architecture remains intact in a mixed residential/commercial area next to the ferry terminal. Boats leave here daily for Quebec's Iles-de-la-Madeleine or Magdalen Islands, 133 kilometres (80 miles) away.

Originally prime real estate, these homes are perched strategically on the cliffs with a view out to sea. Across from the picnic park and a memorial cairn to lost fishermen is the Matthews House, a Victorian mansion now run as an inn. Recently the owners received an award for the restoration of this house. Kitty-corner to it is one of the oldest buildings in Souris, a Georgian-style house built by Donald Beaton, one of the founders of Souris. Other interesting buildings in various states of repair can be seen down by the old movie theatre.

Leave Souris on Route 16 and head toward East Point. A few miles past the turnoff to the ferry begins a beautiful drive through farmland. Off to the right, sometimes close, and sometimes just a glimmering blue in the distance, is Northumberland Strait.

Sticking to this road has its disadvantages. It is not apparent that at the edge of the distant blue, where terra firma crumbles out to meet the sea, is a sand beach that parallels the shore for the next 17 kilometres (10 miles).

Getting to the beach is the problem. There are any number of roads (usually less than a couple of kilometres long), but many of them end up in the backyards of private cottages. Our first opportunity to get to the beach is not well marked, and it is a favorite swimming place for local people.

A few miles out of Souris, watch for a sign that says "St. Catherines Route 303" and then for another that says "Greenvale." Just past here is a red-roofed potato storage barn buried into the hill and a little road to the right. It is paved for a bit but quickly turns to mud. Don't be discouraged by the "No Exit" sign. Follow the red mud road through a patchwork of fields, spruce thickets, and houses and through a salt marsh. The road stops abruptly behind the dunes of Little Harbour. On foot, follow the narrow path that snakes its way through the marram grass down to the beach. And what a beach! Bits of driftwood and bladdered seaweed are all that clutter an otherwise pure stretch of fine, tangerine-tinged sand. Remarkable red cliffs with a brush cut of green trees on top frame the sides of the beach. Every summer P.E.I. is a haven for Nova Scotians and New Brunswickers. In spite of the beauty at home, including dozens of impressive sand beaches, Maritimers come here for the warm water. It's not like their home, where swimming in the North Atlantic is a brief splash and a mad dash back to the hot sands to drum up the courage for another try.

In P.E.I., swimming means sprawling with friends at the water's edge, light summer conversation, and not much else. The tide creeps up without anyone noticing, and the kids won't come out of the water at all.

Now drive back to the corner and turn right. Soon we cross a small river that feeds into Black Pond across the road. Bird-watchers take note: beyond the pond is a combination of dunes and marshland called the Black Pond Bird Sanctuary.

Just up the road is Red Point Provincial Park and another opportunity for us to get down to the never-ending beach.

Being higher in elevation than our last access, the park kindly provides twenty wooden steps down to the sand. From the erosion on the cliffs it looks like others have found a shortcut down by sliding on their backsides—not recommended!

The park is a large, grassy field and doesn't offer much natural foliage for shelter, but it does offer other amenities for campers, including tables, telephones, bathrooms, and playground equipment. Children held captive for too long in the backseats of cars have a need to slide through plastic tubes and hang from monkey bars, and here is their chance.

Turning back to the highway, we observe that this area, or all of P.E.I. for that matter, must be a watercolour artist's dreamland. The sky and clouds are etched with different gradations of grey, blue, and white. The fields are overlapping shades of green, yellow, and brown, ending in smudges of hedges and windrows. In the foreground, the ditches are sprinkled with thousands of little white stars—strawberry blossoms punctuated by yellow dots of dandelions.

Two and a half kilometres (1.5 miles) down Route 16, at Kingsboro, is the turnoff to the Basin Head Fisheries Museum. Turn right at the sign and take the road that parallels a huge tidal pond called Basin Head Harbour. At the museum rent a canoe and paddle this gentle 5-kilometre (3-mile) waterway.

The beach continues the same magnificent stretch of sand. Fresh water gushes through the narrow harbour, which is straddled by a strange hump-backed metal bridge (no jumping off allowed!).

The museum complex includes displays of boats, inshore fishing equipment, lighthouse memorabilia, and native artifacts found on the beach. But more fascinating is the tiny, intimate community of board-and-batten fish stores, lobster cannery, and wharf at the water's edge. Although the fishermen are long gone, their presence remains.

Back at the corner make a right turn and proceed to East Point. The green farmland rolls on. The water becomes just a touch of blue in the corner of the eye. Just past the turnoff to Munn's Road, Route 301, is a red mud road. It's less than a kilometre (half mile) drive down to the beach at the tip of Basin Head Harbour. Used mainly by residents, this lovely spot is a favorite of bird-watchers, as the salt marsh nearby is home to many species of shorebirds.

At East Point follow the sign that reads, "East Point Lighthouse 2 km Turn Right No Exit." The lighthouse is an impressive three-story white wooden structure with an octagonal glass top framed in red. Built in 1867, the 20-metre-high (66-foot-high) building towers above the 11-metre (36-foot) cliffs. The view from the top is awesome, with seals bobbing in the waves below and a host of seabirds swooping and diving.

Most impressive is the spot itself. We brace ourselves at the chain-link fence and observe the sea. This is the easternmost tip of P.E.I. Three massive tidal movements converge here: the Atlantic Ocean, the Gulf of St. Lawrence, and Northumberland Strait. Looking down on the water, we can actually differentiate the wave patterns coming from different directions.

The whitecaps converge to lash away at the land, and the cliffs are raw and abrupt. Some see faces in the cliffs, a spooky sight. The trees, in order to survive, have submitted to the desires of the wind. Stunted and twisted like bonsai, they are permanently bent over, frozen in twisted expressions of horror.

This is a formidable spot. We hike down the trail, westerly along the edge of the cliffs, and down to a sand beach toward Beaton Point. Little children in bathing suits skip down the path here, but for those used to flatter terrain, the heights can be a bit of a challenge.

Back on the main road, take Route 16 west toward North Lake. Huge heaps of sand have washed up along the shore.

Grass poking out of the top gives them a comical touch—they look like baby elephants.

Turn right toward the fishing village of North Lake Harbour. Clustered near the sea inlet of North Lake is a unique community of about 100 working boats. Behind the boats are dozens of tiny compact, turquoise, green, and blue storage sheds and cabins, temporary homes for the owners of the boats. Lobster pots are stacked up neatly beside them. This is one of the largest inshore fishing fleets on P.E.I.

Follow the loop around North Lake, which was a freshwater lake until 1917, when the sea crashed through. Cross the bridge back to Route 16 and within a mile turn right on Route 16A toward Elmira.

Elmira is the appropriate end of the line for our journey. In the middle of a field is what used to be the last station stop for the P.E.I. railway. Now it is a museum.

The discontinued, disconnected railway cars look a bit forlorn sitting in the grass. But the building is joy for those of us who can remember these familiar old station houses with sloping shingled roofs, small-paned windows, and generous platforms.

The large placard reads "ELMIRA." These signs were checked off all along the way by passengers marking their progress on a trip. As the train slowed down into Elmira, the sign also signified the end of the line. Sitting in the pewlike chair on the platform, we feel a strange sense of expectation as if at any moment the train will rumble in and smiling faces will greet us, excited with stories of a visit to Charlottetown.

Meticulously restored by the P.E.I. Heritage Foundation, the station is now a museum. The wood floors are polished and the pot-bellied stove looks primed to heat the place. The rooms are filled with train memorabilia: brass train lanterns, old photos, maps, oil lamps, milk cans, and suitcases. The train roster hangs on the wall.

The station is no longer vitally connected to anything. The tracks have been taken up, and the paths are in the process of being transformed into a 23-kilometre (14-mile) trail for hikers and cross-country ski enthusiasts that goes all the way to Souris. Try out the trail and then come back for a picnic on the lawn and to contemplate the end of an era.

Continue down Route 16A to South Lake, turn right, and drive the main road back to Souris.

In the Area

Basin Head Fisheries Museum (South Lake): 902-357-2966

East Point Lighthouse and Craft Shop (East Point): 902-357-2106

Elmira Railway Museum (Elmira): 902-357-2481

Ferry information:

> Borden–Cape Tormentine, N.B. (Marine Atlantic, North Sydney, N.S.): 902-855-2030

> Wood Islands–Caribou, N.S. (Northumberland Ferries): 800-566-3838 (within Nova Scotia and P.E.I.), 902-566-3838 (elsewhere)

Matthew House Inn (Souris): 902-687-3461

P.E.I. provincial parks:

> Eastern Administration: 902-652-2356

> Red Point (South Lake): 902-357-2463

> Souris Beach: 902-687-3238

Souris Tourist Information Centre: 902-687-3238

Town of Souris: 902-687-2157

Wood Islands Tourist Information Centre: 902-962-2015

6 ~

Northern Queens County and Prince Edward Island National Park

From Charlottetown: Take Route 2 west to Milton. Turn right on Route 7 and less than a mile, turn left on Route 224 to Ebenezer. The 100-kilometre (60-mile) road is a figure eight that goes to Stanley Bridge, Malpeque Bay, and back to Stanley Bridge through the national park, ending at Rustico. Travel time without stops: two hours.

Highlights: *Glasgow Road Gallery, P.E.I. Preserves Company, New London, birthplace of L. M. Montgomery, New London Bay, history of the Yankee Gale, clay roads, Scenic Heritage Road, Cabot Beach Provincial Park, Malpeque, St. Mary's Roman Catholic Church, lobster suppers, Stanley Bridge, P.E.I. National Park, sand dunes, Irish moss, La Banque de Rustico.*

Our second route on P.E.I. takes us over the back roads of Queens County in the north central part of the island. Probably the most interesting area of concentrated beauty on the island, it contains the glorious dunes of P.E.I. National Park and Cavendish, the centre of the "Anne of Green Gables" hoopla.

This is the first destination of most of the 700,000 tourists who visit P.E.I each year. In spite of the inconvenience of the traffic and the carnival-like atmosphere at Cavendish (which children love), we journey there. We cannot leave P.E.I. without seeing what many people consider to be the most beautiful part of the island.

To avoid the crowds, visit any time of the year except the high season, July and August. Many of the hotels give excellent off-season rates. Unfortunately when tourists are not in evidence, neither are the services that cater to them: the information bureaus, restaurants, craft shops, and bed and breakfasts.

Country stores are few and far between. Most residents shop in the cities. We avoid the "nothing open and we're hungry" problem by keeping cookies and fruit in the car. Charlottetown and Summerside are within a one-hour drive of the most remote spot.

The road starting at Ebenezer is 25 kilometres (15 miles) of classic post-card farmland: parallel rows of potatoes snaking up and down, over hill and dale. Behind the cultivated fields, healthy stands of hardwoods add a stunning three-dimensional quality to the view. Driving along this road on a fresh green morning or when the hills are bathed in the golden rays of a setting sun, we notice an intensity not found on other parts of the island, where the land is flatter and not as lush.

Past Wheatley River (2.5 kilometres or 1.5 miles east of New Glasgow) is the Glasgow Road Gallery. Artist Hugh Crosby has converted a barn next to his house into a large gallery. A native Nova Scotian who fell in love with the landscape and slow pace of the island, Crosby seeks off-trail images and details like abandoned barns and wisps of greenery against red soil and translates them onto paper and canvas.

At New Glasgow there is a lovely pastoral spot on the banks of the Clyde River just before we cross the bridge. An old wooden building known locally as "the butter factory" has been converted into the P.E.I. Preserves Company.

It's a good place to stop for tea and a pastry, or a full meal. One unique thing about the establishment is that visitors, standing behind a glass window, can look down on the black-and-white-chequered floor where preserves are being cooked and bottled. The jams and jellies, made from fresh fruits and berries, are sold along with imported teas in crafted gift packages.

Cross the bridge, turn left, then right, to stay on Route 224.

People who come to P.E.I. for a feed of lobster will be happy to know that there's ample opportunity to stop at one of the many lobster suppers found all over the island.

There are fine commercially run suppers at New London and New Glasgow, but for a real community supper, we stop at the St. Ann Church supper, just off Route 224, located in St. Ann on Route 266, about 5 kilometres (3 miles) west of New Glasgow. We walk into the church basement for the finest of feasts prepared by the ladies of the community.

The "all-you-can-eat" dishes are served first; the salads, cheeses, rolls, seafood chowder, mussels, pickles, and relishes are a meal unto themselves. But attempt a little self-discipline here and leave room for the main focus of the feast—the lobster. Diners are covered with a bib before the fiery red crustacean is delivered, all cracked, sliced, and ready to eat. To top off the meal (as if anyone really needs it) is a cornucopia of desserts: pies, crisps, squares, and plates of cake.

The ladies like children. They serve them small portions and offer ham and roast beef as an alternative main course for picky eaters (or let the kids fill up on cake).

On to Stanley Bridge and a sweeping view up New London Bay. At New London, turn right on Route 20 to Springbrook and French River. There's a good lunch stop here called the Kitchen Witch. Friends who live in the neighborhood recommend their breakfasts of farm fresh eggs, toasted home-made bread, and jam.

New London was called Clifton when Lucy Maud Mont-gomery, author of *Anne of Green Gables* (1908), was born here in 1874. She lived here for the first few years of her life before moving to Cavendish to live with her grandparents. The mod-est, green-trimmed wooden home is a provincial historic site and museum, open to the public. On display are some of her treasured personal effects: her wedding dress, personal scrap-books, and a replica of the blue chest that appears in *The Story Girl* (1911).

The Mi'kmaq called New London Bay *Kicheboogwek Book-taba*, which means "enclosed bay." This is a good description of this harbour, which is almost entirely sealed off by the 7-kilometre-long (4-mile-long) Cavendish sandspit. In the early 1800s, before the advent of roads, the communities of French River/New London and Cavendish were close. Faith-fully, every Sunday, in winter, spring, summer, and fall, the residents of Cavendish would trek to the end of the sandspit and catch a ferryboat across the narrow channel to the New London side for church services.

Relaxing on the shore next to this gently sloping bay, we might infer that the relationship between men, women, and the sea has been an easy one. But for another point of view explore a fascinating cemetery in French River, which dates back to the early 1800s. The Yankee Hill cemetery contains the graves of twenty-five American sailors drowned during the "Yankee Gale" of 1851.

At that time mackerel fishing in the Gulf of St. Law-rence was so rich that hundreds of fishing boats from Port-land, Gloucester, and Boston sailed this far north to share in the bounty. On October 3, 1851, a gale arose, combining a huge downpour and an exceptionally high tide. Captains of

71

American schooners berthed in small harbours sensed the danger and headed out to sea in an attempt to round North Cape to safety.

The tide rose, sweeping away bridges and dams. Crops were destroyed, and barns, houses, and large trees were blown over. From Cape North to East Point, seventy-four ships with 160 persons onboard were wrecked against the shore. The bodies that washed ashore were buried in the Yankee Hill Cemetery, as well as at Malpeque, Stanhope, and other plots.

Back on Route 20 and less than a mile down the road, we have the option of turning right on the unpaved road that leads to the New London Lighthouse. This lookoff has one of the best views of the Cavendish sandspit. Great blue heron and cormorants are commonly seen here in the summer.

The one impediment to reaching the New London Lighthouse is the unpaved road, or "clay road," as they are called here. They can't be called gravel roads because P.E.I. is agriculturally blessed with an almost rock-free soil.

Island dirt has not a bit of grit in it. When the "spring" rains come, which can be anytime between March and June, the unpaved roads do not turn to chili (like other places in the Maritimes). Driving down a slick and greasy, rain-saturated clay road in P.E.I., especially one gouged by heavy farm machinery, can be likened to boating through applesauce.

We prefer a nice hike down this lovely lane to the shore. The roadside brims with fragrant purple lupines and daisies. The sky is wide and clear, and we have peace of mind knowing that we won't have to ask a farmer to pull us out of the muck.

At the corner either backtrack to the main road or follow the shore on a short clay road called Cape Road, which meets the pavement a few miles down the shore.

Cape Road is a lovely country lane with the ambience of the island fifty years ago—saltwater farms and fields that stretch down to the grey blue gulf. Cape Tryon is on this road.

It's worth the hike to the lighthouse for the view from the top of a 35-metre (115.5-foot) cliff. One of the island's largest cormorant colonies nests here.

Back on the pavement, head toward Campbell's Pond. For *Anne of Green Gables* fans, there is a museum at Park Corner, the home of L. M. Montgomery's uncle, John Campbell. It was the model for some of the scenes in Montgomery's books, including the Lake of Shining Waters, just across the road. First editions of the Anne books are displayed in the drawing room where she was married in 1911.

At Park Corner we take a little detour to explore a road designated as a "Scenic Heritage Road." These narrow clay roads have been identified (and described in a pamphlet) by the province and the Island Nature Trust. They are protected from removal of vegetation and other "improvements." It's probably not a good idea to try this road in rainy weather from March until mid-June.

Turn left on Route 101 to Irishtown and drive for about 5 kilometres (3 miles) to Route 233, where we turn right on the County Line Road. This road straddles the Prince/Queens County border. According to the pamphlet, the summit of the hill on this road provides a spectacular view of the Gulf of St. Lawrence to the north and the rolling hills to the south. Interestingly, this secluded trail was a favorite of rumrunners en route to Kensington from the shore.

"It is reported to be so steep at the base," the pamphlet reads, "that a wagon driver with a load of grain (or rum for that matter) could touch the ears of his horses while sitting in his seat!"

At the corner return to the pavement of Route 20 and turn left toward Sea View (where there isn't much of one) and onto Darnley.

The Darnley Basin is inaccessible from this road. Unlike some areas where any back road that leads to the water is

73

worth exploring, the roads down to the shore here are not recommended. They are undependable in rainy weather and often lead down to a cow pasture or a cottage subdivision.

Turn right at Malpeque to Cabot Beach Provincial Park, a landscape of interesting contrasts. Next to the park, a tangle of fishermen's sheds and gear is counterposed by sand dunes shimmering silver-green in the afternoon sun. Following a hiking trail through the spruce-fragrant and intimate woods of the park, we can hear the roar of the surf long before we see it. On the beach next to the sandstone cliffs the fresh salt air and a swirl of seagulls whip around us.

This 1,600-hectare (4,000-acre) peninsula, of which the park takes up about one-quarter, is bounded on three sides by the waters of March Water, Richmond Bay, and the Darnley Basin and has an interesting history. Although the British tried to rename the region Princetown, the original Mi'kmaq name, *Makpaak*, which means "big bay," has lingered on. The British had great plans for this area. In 1765 surveyor Samuel Holland divided the whole island into lots to facilitate the disposal of land by ballot, chiefly to military and naval officers. He set aside three "royalties" or town sites, one for each county: Georgetown in Kings County, Charlottetown in Queens County, and Princetown in Prince County.

Princetown simply never evolved. Summerside was situated in a better position and became the commercial centre for the county.

In October 1770, the first group of 200 British settlers arrived in a brigantine called the *Annabella* from Campbelltown, Kintyre, Scotland. Expecting a town with streets, squares, and common pasture land, they were shocked to discover almost total wilderness. To make matters worse, after they had safely rowed ashore, an intense snow squall began to blow. The ship broke free and was lost with much of its cargo. Only through the generosity of Mi'kmaq and Acadians did the settlers survive the first winter. In 1964 a granite cairn to the Scottish settlers was placed near the entrance to the park on the site of an old burying ground.

Leaving the park, follow the signs past potato conveyors back to Route 20, past the war memorial and Princetown United Church toward Kensington. At Baltic turn right, following the shore toward Hamilton and loop back toward Indian River. Gentle fields flow down to the shore of Oyster Cove and Chichester Cove.

In Indian River the red-roofed, white-spired St. Mary's Roman Catholic Church rises dramatically out of the farmland. This church was designed by William Critchlow Harris in 1902 and is in the process of being restored by the community. A dozen wooden carvings of the saints in robes and holding crosses grace the top of the spire. The graveyard is much older than the church (1850s) and will be of interest to people researching their English/Irish/Scottish Catholic roots in this area.

Follow Route 20 to Kensington and turn left on Route 6 to Margate. Turn right at the church and graveyard, crossing the Queens County border. The Southwest River is off to the left and coming up soon is the "Welcome to Clinton" sign. We're heading back toward New London and on to Cavendish. (It's hard to get lost with all these signs!)

The road meanders through the hilly farmland of the river valley, and the beauty and pristine light conspire to make us want to stop the car and just stare. From our elevated vista we see, off in the distance, a first glimpse of the red cliffs eroded by the Gulf of St. Lawrence.

Go straight through New London, past L. M. Montgomery's birthplace; pottery, craft, and antique shops; churches; the town barber shop, the firehall, and some nice old homes.

At Stanley Bridge, cross the Stanley River where it feeds into placid, lakelike New London Bay. Here, the great blue herons seem to have gotten quite used to gawking at humanity. Watching them lift into the air is a thrill—they look like flapping pterodactyls.

If the weather is rainy, stay on Route 6 to Cavendish. If the weather's decent, we have an alternate route on a clay road to the national park. It was a tip shared with us by a resident. He describes it as "a lovely way to avoid the strip" of commercial enterprise.

After crossing the bridge over the Stanley River do not turn left on Route 6, but keep straight on Route 224 for 3 kilometres (2 miles), where we turn left to Hope River. The

Fishing boats near the Stanley Bridge

road is paved part of the way, then turns to clay. The drive can be compared to a roller-coaster ride. We descend into the gully of the trickling creek and then ride high at the crest of the hill, where we can see all the way to New London Bay. When this road meets Route 6, turn right toward Cavendish and proceed for 1.25 kilometres (.75 mile), and then take a left toward the shore. This diversion leads right to the dunes of Prince Edward Island National Park.

The more commercial aspects of Cavendish can be discovered just down the road. Stay on Route 6 for the Green Gables House, Cranberry Village, Enchanted Castle, Grandpa's Antique Photo Studio, King Tut's Tomb and Treasures, Rainbow Valley Amusement Park, Ripley's Believe It or Not! Museum, Royal Atlantic Wax Museum, Sandspit Amusements, or the site of Lucy Maud Montgomery's Cavendish home, and much, much more.

Now on to Prince Edward Island National Park. It's hard to find the words to describe this shore. We sense the overwhelming emotions that national parks biologists must have felt in 1937 when they stood atop the 6-metre (20-foot) dunes and sandstone cliffs of this fragile coastline and declared it a national treasure worth protecting for all time.

From one perspective, this park doesn't need protecting. If anyone has the upper hand here, it is Mother Nature, who goes about her business oblivious to human activity. Four-and-a-half-metre (15-foot) heaps of sand drift onto the roads and have to be repeatedly bulldozed aside. Breaker after breaker, an infinity of waves crashes on the shore, not caring that hundreds or even thousands of people may be sitting mesmerized by the rhythm of the waters.

After washing ashore, the sand blows away in a dusty wind or is washed back out to sea, unless it is captured by a beach weed called marram grass. The grass grows in clumps and spreads by underground runners, which send lifelines to

77

new clumps. The plants and runners form a net that protects the sand from the relentless wind and surf.

As tough as the grass is, it is also fragile. The roots, which grow in loose sand, have little to protect them from trampling human feet and, even worse, vehicles. Once the root system is damaged, the sand is free to scatter in the wind. A notch created like this is called a "blowout." For this reason guests of the park are requested to stick to the boardwalks.

Swimming at Cavendish and Rustico Beach is divine from the middle of July until September, when the water temperature stays around 25°C (72°F). It's possible to out-distance the worst of the crowds by walking down to the end of the sandspit.

The high dunes that L. M. Montgomery nicknamed the Watch-Tower are long gone. Erosion has eaten away 100 metres (330 feet) of dunes since then.

If the land is fragile, the sea is mindless and unforgiving. Hundreds of ships have been dashed to pieces near these seemingly friendly beaches, against offshore sandbars, sand-spits, and rocky ledges.

When humanity stakes any claim to this land it cannot do so with much security. A tempestuous hurricane can gouge and reshape miles of coastline in a few hours.

Signs deny automobile access to the shore except for Irish moss harvesting. Irish moss is *Chondrus crispus*, a delicate red alga, which, when processed, releases a substance called carrageenan. It can be found in the list of ingredients in ice cream, where it inhibits the formation of ice crystals. It is also used in everything from chocolate milk to toothpaste as a suspending or clarifying agent.

Traditionally, Irish moss was raked off the beaches into horse-drawn carts or dragged from the sea into small boats. In old recipes Irish moss is cooked in milk and sugar until the carrageenan thickens the mixture into a custard.

The view is outstanding at Orby Head and Cape Turner. Here the headlands are very susceptible to erosion, and up to 5 metres (16.5 feet) of coastline disappear every year. The faces of sandstone rock formations are constantly changing at the whims of the sculpting sea. Far to the right, past the fishing boats and birds, is a strip of coastline—the other half of the national park. Cape Turner is a great place to stop for a picnic and more of the view.

At Rollings Pond, Route 6 turns sharply to the right through North Rustico, a small fishing community. The charming scale of this village has made it a haven for photographers.

La Banque de Rustico (Farmers Bank of Rustico) (1864-1894) is an interesting historic building. Constructed of red island sandstone blocks and island timber, the hand-hewn beams were pinned together with dowels and pegs, entirely without nails.

Equally as interesting as the structure is the history of the building. Under the leadership of Father Georges-Antoine Belcourt, the Acadian farmers of Rustico opened their own "people's bank" in 1864. Measured by capital, it was the smallest bank ever chartered in Canada. It dispensed loans and had its own notes illustrated with the pastoral etching of a farmer guiding a hand plow behind two horses. The bank did well, but when P.E.I. entered the Confederation in 1873, the British North America Act gave sole control of banking to the federal government. They put the small banks out of business in favor of big banks with large capital and cross-country branches. The bank eventually died, but not before a fight lasting twenty years. The Farmers Bank of Rustico is said to have been the spiritual precursor to the *caisses populaires*, or cooperative credit societies of Quebec, and later, the credit unions of Canada and the United States.

To see the other half of Prince Edward Island National Park, stay on Route 6 to Brackley Beach.

To return to Charlottetown, leave North Rustico and turn right on Route 269 to Mayfield. At Mayfield turn left on Route 13 toward New Glasgow. Route 13 is a beautiful river drive to the town of Hunter River and Route 2. Turn left to Charlottetown or right to Summerside.

In the Area

La Banque de Rustico (Farmers Bank of Rustico) (Rustico): 902-963-2505

Cavendish/Rusticoville Tourist Information Centre: 902-963-2639

Glasgow Road Gallery (Wheatley River): 902-964-3465

The Island Nature Trust (Charlottetown): 902-566-9150, 892-7513

Kitchen Witch Tea Room (Long River): 902-886-2294

Lucy Maud Montgomery Birthplace (New London): 902-886-2099

New Glasgow lobster suppers: 902-964-2870

New London lobster suppers: 902-886-2599

Prince Edward Island National Park, Canadian Parks Service Information, summer: 902-963-2391, winter: 902-672-6350

Prince Edward Island Museum and Heritage Foundation (Charlottetown): 902-892-9127

Prince Edward Island Preserves Company (New Glasgow): 902-964-2524

St. Ann lobster suppers: 902-964-2385

St. Mary's Roman Catholic Church (Indian River): 902-836-3733

NOVA SCOTIA

VSHERIDAN©1994

7 ~

Nature in the Extreme:

The Parrsboro Shore

From Truro: Take the Trans-Canada Highway (Highway 104) 17 kilometres (10 miles) to exit 11, and west on Route 2 to Great Village.

From Amherst: Take the Trans-Canada Highway (Highway 104) west to exit 11. The road goes for 100 kilometres (60 miles) from Great Village near the eastern end of Cobequid Bay, along the Minas Basin, through the town of Parrsboro and west to Advocate Harbour.

Highlights: *Great Village, Upper Economy, Dutchman Cheese Shop and Tearoom, Five Islands Provincial Park, Glooscap, Parrsboro, fossils, rock collecting, Rockhound Roundup, Ship's Company Theatre, Spencers Island, Glooscap's Kettle, Mary Celeste, Cape d'Or, Advocate Harbour, Joggins.*

Our trip begins on the eastern side of Great Village where, looking across farmers' fields, we get a glimpse of Cobequid Bay. The water will always be on our left and evolves from Cobequid Bay to Minas Basin and finally Minas Channel.

Great Village, a charming village of 500 people, features some very old and interesting buildings in various states of repair. The widow's walks, towers, gables, mansard roofs, and gingerbread indicate that they were built during more prosperous times of the past. A hundred years ago, the village

83

hummed with activity. Lumber, pulp wood, iron, and steel from the Londonderry Iron Works were loaded on local wharves and shipped out to world markets.

The Great Village elementary school is a striking building. Robert Layton's Store (circa 1870), which has been in the Layton family for three generations, was recently designated a Provincial Heritage Property.

The store sells the usual cold drinks, snacks, and groceries. But a room in the back has been set aside as a country-store museum. Old inventory from the store has been placed on display: china, a wicker dress form, hat pins, bolts of cloth, high-buttoned shoes, Comfort soap, thread, a butter press, and saddle nails.

Across the street is St. James United Church (circa 1883). The imposing gothic structure, with a majestic 40-metre (112-foot) steeple, has flamboyant corner buttresses and interior double hammer-beam ceilings of varnished wood. While most country churches of this vintage were designed and built by parish carpenters, this church was professionally designed by architect James Charles Dumaresq, whose descendants still practice in Halifax.

A few miles past Great Village is Highland Village, where miles of fertile shore were reclaimed by the Acadian dykes hundreds of years ago. The prominent ridge at the water's edge is evidence of the hand-built dykes that continue to hold back the world's highest tides. The land across the bay is the Noel Shore.

Near the Portapique River is an artist's studio and gallery called Watercolours by Joy Laking. Her realistic paintings of salt marsh, flowers, and farmhouses are reflections of her rural life. The gallery is open year-round by chance or by appointment.

Bass River is a quaint little river town. For a closer look at the bay, take one of two roads on either side of the river to King's Rest or Saint's Rest.

At Upper Economy we pass the remains of a World War II gunnery tower. This wooden structure is Nova Scotia's answer to the Leaning Tower of Pisa. Also in Upper Economy is the Dutchman Cheese Shop and "Deel" Tearoom, where the Van Den Hoek family produces and sells first-class Gouda by the pound or wheel. Open during the tourist season, the tearoom features homemade soups, sandwiches, pizza, and its dessert specialty, *appeltaart*. The outside deck looks out across the water to Burntcoat, Hants County, which is purported to have the highest tides (16.3 metres or 54 feet) on the Minas shore.

At Upper Economy the landscape changes dramatically. The flat farmland ascends into the hills. The pebbled beaches turn to red sands fronting on red-faced cliffs. Even the soil in the ditches is rust coloured.

Seven kilometres (4 miles) down the road, at Carr's Brook, we look out on a spit of land—Economy Mountain. At sunset, when the light is just right, an optical illusion tricks us into thinking that the land is floating above the water.

From here the road quickly climbs Economy Mountain (also called Gerrish Mountain) to a height of 182 metres (600 feet) above sea level. Behind us is one of the most dramatic views on this road. It is good incentive for us to come back this way for the descending view.

At the top of the mountain (with popping ears) the valleys sweep down on two sides. Soon we start to descend into the luxurious birch forest. Through a break in the trees we get a glimmer of the five islands for which the next village, Five Islands, is aptly named.

Five Islands and the next 50 kilometres (30 miles) to Advocate Harbour is one of the most exhilarating motoring landscapes in Nova Scotia. For children with a fascination for pebbles and a passion for dinosaurs, for renowned geologists, gemologists, and paleontologists, this is the most exciting place in the world. On this journey, millions of years of geological time open up in the sandstone and basalt cliffs.

Forget for a moment puny human time counted in hundreds of years for European settlers and tens of thousands of years for aboriginal peoples. Now contemplate earth time, 300 million years ago, when Africa and North America were joined together in one supercontinent called Pangaea. Nova Scotia was where central Mexico is today.

The land beneath where we stand was a tropical rain forest. Two hundred million years ago (this is the theory) a 10-kilometre-wide (6-mile-wide) asteroid slammed into the earth near Maznicouagan, Quebec, with a force 10,000 times more powerful than the modern world's entire nuclear stockpile. The earth went into convulsions. Volcanoes spewed, skies darkened, and 40 percent of animal life perished. The floating solid plates of the earth's crust were split and gouged, separating the continents and forming the Bay of Fundy.

The tropical forests were deluged with hot liquid volcanic rock. In time, the vegetation compressed into coal, preserving imprints of the animals crushed within. The lava cooled into shiny and sometimes frothy rocks. Where gases were trapped in the igneous rock, holes formed and liquid percolating through them grew into delicate crystals.

The earth's crust is made up of thousands of layers of mineral, vegetable, and animal matter laid down over the millennia like a perfectly ordered record book.

What is so extraordinary about the Parrsboro shore is that a vertical gash, or fault, has been cut through the horizontal layers, opening a window into the pages of time. Like a huge knife, the unrelenting 15-metre (50-foot) tides of the Bay of Fundy continue to slice away at the coast, revealing new treasures every spring. To appreciate this, a person really has to get down to the beaches for a close look at the cliffs. Adventurous gem seekers (otherwise known as rockhounds) will go to any length to scale the cliffs. They leave behind remnants of fishermen's ropes tied to trees where they have gone over the edge to inspect rock faces. They keep tide tables and cold chisels on their persons at all times and wear three pairs of socks inside their hiking boots to avoid sprains on rubble beaches.

But for the less hardy and ambitious, there are other ways down to the beach. Roads have been cut along the mountain streams that drain into the basin. It is essential to get off the main road (Routes 2 and 209) at least a couple of times, not only to inspect the sea cliffs, but also to experience the spectacular widening perspective of water, islands, and beyond.

Our first opportunity to get to the water is at Five Islands Provincial Park. A paved road emerges through the thick forest on the shore at the back of Moose Island, whose hump looks like the giant beast emerging from the water. The string of islands, composed of basalt, were once one long finger of resistant volcanic rock. Swirling tides and currents gradually eroded weaknesses, leaving an archipelago of islands with mysterious caves and basalt sea stacks. The other four islands are called Pinnacle, Diamond, Long, and Egg. When the tide is out, they seem close enough to touch. Although they seem a short hike away because of the tides, it is not recommended that people visit them except by boat.

One dramatic hiking trail in the park leads to Red Head, where the cliffs at the water's edge (the base of Economy Mountain) reveal rusty red petrified sand dunes capped with black basalt and greyish white limestone trickling down.

This is an awe-inspiring and, some would say, even magical place. Standing tens of metres above the boiling surf, on the edge of a cliff where one slip would be our last, is a humbling experience. So is walking the beach, where steep cliff overhangs are beautiful, but should be avoided without a hard hat. Ambling onto a mudflat where the incoming tide chases us back as fast, or faster, than we can run, makes us respect the raw power of nature.

There is a native tale explaining the creation of these islands by Glooscap, a cultural hero in Mi'kmaq mythology. As the story goes, when the mischievous Beaver taunted his people, Glooscap flung clods of earth at him, forming the five islands.

The Mi'kmaq Indians, who lived here long before the European settlers, were culturally aligned with Algonquian-speaking natives of the East Coast. Marion Robertson, in her book *Red Earth: Tales of the Micmacs*, describes Glooscap as an invulnerable character with a miraculous birth and childhood. He performed great deeds and taught the people all they know. The existence of many natural phenomena in the Maritimes is explained as the work of Glooscap. The story of Glooscap's departure is that he did not die, but will return when the people have great need of him.

The 440-hectare (1,100-acre) park features a campground, picnic park, beach, over 13 kilometres (8 miles) of scenic hiking trails, and interpretive signs. During the snowy months, two of the inland trails are used as cross-country ski trails.

Follow Route 2 through wooded hills to Parrsboro. This harbour at low tide is an unusual sight. The boats sit high and dry on the mud flats and the water is kilometres away.

The tourist bureau on Main Street offers a wealth of information about the area. It's worth exploring the two branching side roads, each 8 or 10 kilometres (5 or 6 miles) long, on opposite sides of Parrsboro Harbour. The east side road to Greenhill has a magnificent view of Cape Split and the Blomidon Peninsula. It's quite a surprise to see how close we are to the Wolfville shore (about 8 kilometres, or 5 miles, as the crow flies) when our sense of distance has been prejudiced by the overland route of 310 kilometres (185 miles).

The road on the west side of the harbour leads to a favorite tourist spot, historic Ottawa House, formerly owned by Prime Minister Charles Tupper and presently a museum. Partridge Island, now connected to the mainland by a tombolo, is probably the most accessible beach for rock collecting. Rock collectors of all ages are almost guaranteed to find agates and zeolites.

Near the centre of Parrsboro is an unusual tent-covered boat. This is the Ship's Company Theatre, which all summer long brings the magic of the stage to the deck of the MV *Kipawo*, the last ferryboat to sail from Wolfville to Parrsboro. Its name is a peculiar combination of the names Kingsport, Parrsboro, and Wolfville. The company performs plays celebrating local history and folklore by Maritime writers such as Harry Thurston as well as pieces by international playwrights such as Athol Fugard. It is a good idea to phone ahead for tickets to these accomplished productions.

Rock collectors will want to visit the Nova Scotia Museum's Fundy Geological Museum (newly constructed in 1993) and Parrsboro Rock and Mineral Shop, run by local expert Eldon George. On display are outstanding samples of fossils, minerals, and crystals including agate (the provincial gemstone), amethyst, jasper, and zeolite (including stillbite, the Nova Scotia provincial mineral). For people who aren't lucky on the beaches, George sells all kinds of rocks at reasonable prices.

Visitors will want to ask for advice about when and where to look for gems and fossils as well as information on the strict provincial guidelines for collectors. Certain areas are protected. Individuals are usually permitted to pick fossil fragments off the beach, but it is forbidden to chisel samples out of the cliffs. Fossil field trips and harbour cruises are popular and guarantee visitors breathtaking views and bona fide fossils.

The Parrsboro area is one of the hottest fossil spots in North America (particularly Wassons Bluff on the Greenhill Road near Two Islands).

In 1984, Eldon George was seeking shelter under a rock outcropping when he noticed a small pool of water seventy-five millimetres (three inches) deep. In the bottom he saw what looked like dinosaur footprints and after a little picking away at the rock he uncovered twenty-eight perfect three-toed 12.5-millimetre-long (half-inch-long) footprints of the world's smallest dinosaur.

In 1986 Columbia University geologist Paul Olsen and Harvard University biologist Neil Shubin found a dinosaur-bone bed several thousand metres from George's footprints. Unearthed were more than 100,000 pieces of fossilized bone, including thirteen skulls and jaws of tritheledonts, cat-sized reptiles that are the closest known relatives of mammals.

Rock collecting reaches a frenzied pitch at the annual Rockhound Roundup, a community celebration held annually during the second week in August since 1966. Besides guided collecting trips, there are rock/mineral/fossil identification classes, lapidary demonstrations, and much more. For the beginner, classes can be very useful. Agate on the beach doesn't look at all like the polished jewel found in shops. Geologists teach amateurs to look for warty-looking waxy lumps—gas bubbles in hardened lava called amygdules.

Leaving Parrsboro, follow Route 209 to Diligent River, through the towns of Fox River, Port Greville, Ward's Brook, Brookville, and Fraserville.

The road is an asphalt path that snakes its way up and down the mountains. We are forced to make more than one hairpin turn as it plunges into a creek bed. The speed signs scare us down to about 16 kilometres (10 miles) per hour.

The roads have definitely not been designed for those of us who want to breeze in and out of here in a few hours. These roads must have been an afterthought.

Most of the human comings and goings on this shore, until recently, were not overland but by sea. The Mi'kmaq got around for thousands of years on foot and by canoe. The Europeans arrived in creaky wooden boats and settled wherever a break in the cliffs would allow, usually on the flat outwash at the mouths of brooks. In time thousands of boats were built on this shore and relations with communities across the basin were closer than with those farther inland.

We take our time on this road. There's a nice picnic spot at Fox River. The paved road is less than 1.6 kilometres (1 mile) off the main road to a beach with shiny conglomerate rocks and a dramatic view of Blomidon and Cape Split.

At Spencers Island we take a short .4-kilometre (.25-mile) drive down a pleasant side street that ends smack dab on the shores of Greville Bay. What a striking spot! The sand is an unexpected charcoal colour. Off to the right is another one of the high-standing hardwood-covered islands unique to this shore, named, obviously, Spencers Island.

This offshore island is also called Glooscap's Kettle. One legend relates how Glooscap left the Mi'kmaq after the white men came. He spent his last winter with his people at Cape d'Or, and after eating his last meal, he left his cooking kettle overturned as this small round island. He transformed to stone his two dogs sitting on their haunches and left them there to guard his kettle. The story concludes on a sad note. After Glooscap left, the animals could no longer speak one language nor walk together as they had when he lived with them.

A cairn near the beach is dedicated to a brigantine, the *Mary Celeste*, built near here. In 1872 it sailed out of New York City destined for Genoa, Italy, but was found drifting in the mid-Atlantic without a soul onboard. The crew of ten, including the captain's wife and baby, had disappeared without a trace. Although the ship's papers and chronometer were missing, everything else was in place, including the woman's sewing next to her chair. The mystery has never been solved.

Five kilometres (3 miles) west on Route 209, is the turnoff to Cape d'Or. Here's a chance to stand high above the crashing surf, tens of metres on top of a knife-edged ledge, with only the lighthouse and blaring foghorn for company.

In order to explore Cape d'Or a traveller needs an afternoon or more to spend in the Advocate area. The drive includes 7 kilometres (4 miles) of rough gravel roads (best not travelled before the spring grading has taken place) up one side of a mountain and back down the other. Then there's a hike down the embankment to the final reward: a pinnacle from which to watch the waters of Advocate Bay and Minas Channel merging with the waters of the Bay of Fundy.

Cape d'Or (Golden Cape) was named by the French explorers for the rocks that they observed glistening in the sun as they approached by boat. Gold, however, proved to be copper, and eventually a mining town was built at nearby Horseshoe Cove. Driving through the woods we'd never guess that civilization (complete with a hotel and dance hall) ever encroached here. Gaping shafts in the forest floor are all that remains of the mine, so it's best to stick to the well-travelled paths.

From the turnoff to Cape d'Or, follow the road through East Advocate, Advocate Harbour, Point Hill, and on to West Advocate. The elements to sum up our journey along the Parrsboro Shore are all here. There is the sweeping view of

Low tide at Advocate Harbour

Advocate Bay with the twin 136-metre (450-foot) cliffs of Cape d'Or and Cape Chignecto on both sides, framing the crescent-shaped vista. Five kilometres (3 miles) of barrier beach almost seal in the harbour except for the influence of the freshwater brooks, which are gentle counterforces to the massive tides. The driftwood on the beach is not a gentle line of twigs and branches but a twisted tangle of roots, limbs, seaweed, and trees, torn full-grown from the cliffs and swallowed up. After all, this is the Bay of Fundy.

A note on Joggins, which because of its geological connection is included here: the road between Advocate Harbour and Joggins is 40 kilometres (25 miles) of alder brush. Except for a welcome break at Apple River, the drive is not a pretty one. To its credit, the road is newly paved.

Joggins has been an internationally famous fossil site since 1851, when Sir Charles Lyell (a colleague of Charles Darwin) and Sir William Dawson, a famous Canadian geologist, discovered it.

Arriving at Joggins, a small town of 600, follow the signs to the cliffs. There is a parking lot a short walk away from the creek gorge where twenty steps lead us down to the beach.

Sealed in sedimentary rock is the life of a 300-million-year-old coastal swamp comparable to today's Florida everglades. Obvious layers or rock strata, which were originally horizontal, are now tilted to the south at a twenty-degree angle. Walking in a northerly direction up the beach, we pass by increasingly older rocks, looking back in geological time. The layers reveal ancient river channels and river plains.

The most obvious fossils are the lycopods, which look like large 9-metre-wide (3-foot-wide) tree stumps. They are actually related to our modern club mosses and the calamites and were the 4.5- to 6-metre (15- to 20-foot) ancestors of current-day horsetails. When these plants died, tiny reptiles and amphibians trapped in the stumps were also preserved.

For more information, consult Laing Ferguson's excellent booklet, *The Fossil Cliffs of Joggins*. It is also interesting to note that the sandstones of this area were used for grindstones, having just the right amount of grit in them. The more finely grained reddish sandstones were used for buildings, including the Province House in Halifax.

In the Area

Layton's General Store (Great Village): 902-668-2022

St. James United Church (Great Village): 902-668-2360

Watercolours by Joy Laking (Portapique River): 902-647-2816

Van Den Hoek Cheese Shop and Tea Room
(Upper Economy): 902-647-2751

Five Islands Provincial Park: 902-254-2980

Parrsboro Tourist Bureau: 902-254-3266

Parrsboro Rock and Mineral Shop (Whitehall Road):
902-254-2981

Ship's Company Theatre (Parrsboro): 902-254-2003, Box
Office: 902-254-3000; within Nova Scotia:
1-800-565-SHOW

Joggins Tourist Bureau: 902-251-2825

8 ~

Blomidon

Country:

Wolfville and
the
Dyke Lands

From Halifax: Take Route 102 north to Bedford, for 13.3 kilometres (8 miles) to Route 101 for 66.6 kilometres (40 miles) to exit 10 to Grand Pré.

From Digby: Take Route 101 east for 133.3 kilometres (80 miles) to exit 10. The road goes for 33.3 kilometres (20 miles) from Grand Pré through Wolfville, across the dyke lands to Blomidon and the Lookoff. Travel time without stops: one hour.

Highlights: *Grand Pré National Historic Site, Cape Blomidon, the dyke lands, semipalmated sandpipers, Evangeline Beach, swimming in the Minas Basin, tides, Covenanter Church, Wolfville, chimney swifts, farm markets, historic apples.*

Our tour starts, strangely enough, in a parking lot. Follow the signs to Grand Pré National Historic Site. But before becoming immersed in the interpretation centre and the stone memorial church, we park the car, walk to the back corner of the lot, and breathe in the view.

Twelve hundred hectares (3,000 acres) of table-flat expanse spread out before us—a rare sight in the Maritimes, except on a dead calm sea. Our vision is filled not with the land, but mostly the sky.

Across the dyke land is an imposing mountain form—Cape Blomidon. Turning ninety degrees to the right, down and away into the distance we see a tiny metal cross. Beyond it is an elm tree, minute from our perspective, but actually a 45-metre-tall (150-foot-tall) giant.

Blomidon's face, the Acadian Cross, and the Planters' Elm: with one pivot we have scanned the three powerful images of this area, which even today are integrated into people's lives.

Cape Blomidon, an imposing promontory with its flat green top and abrupt red cliffs, is the end of the North Mountain Range, which frames one side of the Annapolis Valley for 210 kilometres (125 miles). It is said to be the home of the mythical Mi'kmaq god Glooscap. The mountain ridge simply stops, sloping down to the greedy waves that continually eat away at its soft sandstone face. Blomidon is always there. It is almost as if we could reach out and touch it. Before our drive is over, we will.

The iron cross marks the spot where, in 1755, 5,000 Acadians were wrenched from their homes, marched out under armed guard, and herded onto ships to be scattered along the Eastern Seaboard. Historian George Frederick Clarke writes that as the poor exiles passed the entrance to the Minas Basin, they could see the smoke rising from the roofs of their homes, including 686 buildings, eleven mills, and two churches.

Although the cross marks a point on what was the shore in 1755, today it sits high and dry in the middle of a farmer's field. That is where the historic tide line used to be hundreds of years before modern dykes were built.

Story has it that the old elm tree at Horton Landing at the mouth of the Gaspereau River (now in the middle of Fred Curry's dairy farm) was there when a new group of settlers landed ten years after the Acadians were deported. These were the Planters, recruited from New England by the British. Their settlement was first known as Horton. Later the habitation was called Mud Creek, because of the silted water of their harbour. (It was considered the smallest registered harbour in the world.) In 1830 the name was changed to Wolfville, in recognition of the prominent DeWolfe family.

Both the cross and the elm have been depicted in paintings by noted local painter Alex Colville. His images can be found at Wolfville's bookstore The Box of Delights, or on summer exhibit at Acadia University's Beveridge Arts Centre on Highland Avenue, within walking distance of downtown Wolfville.

The iron cross and the lone elm tree can be viewed at closer range by driving on back lanes through hayfields, through pear and apple orchards, and past stables and chicken barns. Keeping the dyke on our left, with a mind to heading back to the Grand Pré National Historic Site, we can't get lost.

Built on what is believed to be the site of the original Acadian village, the historic setting includes a memorial church of French design and a bronze statue of the fictional character Evangeline of Longfellow's narrative poem. Ironically, the poem, written by an American, did much to stir up feelings of national pride in the dispersed Acadians, which later contributed to the development of this park.

Of interest to gardeners are the grand weeping willows on the edge of the pond. Wendy Elliott, a local journalist, writes, "Although nobody can state categorically that the old French willows date back to cuttings the French settlers brought with them centuries before, they do have a strong emotional significance for many people." A few years ago the park received a request from a Cajun museum in Texas for cuttings of these willows because they grow on the land of the original Acadian village. As a symbol of international friendship, forty cuttings were shipped and planted near the home of Capt. Beausoleil Brossard. Grand Pré is an important touchstone in the collective memory of the Acadian people.

The Church at Grande Pré National Park

Visitors who want to explore the dyke lands can follow a 5-kilometre (3-mile) hiking/biking trail, which begins behind the stone church and leads all the way to Wolfville. The spire of Acadia University acts as a walker's guidepost. Other hiking options originating in the town can be found in the *Self-Guided Walking Trail of the Dykelands,* which is available at the tourist bureau just off Main Street.

Bird-watchers please note: If it is mid-July to mid-September (and especially August), there is an interesting detour in our trip at this point. Leaving the historic site parking lot, turn right and travel 3 kilometres (2 miles) across the fields, following the signs to Evangeline Beach. In its heyday, this old-fashioned resort featured a hotel and, of course, a dance hall. Today only private cottages and a trailer park remain. When the tide is just right people swim here, but the main reason for being here is the birds.

Over a million migrating shorebirds (including over 100,000 semipalmated sandpipers) arrive in the Minas Basin for the purpose of storing up enough energy to survive the nonstop flight to South America, which can take anywhere from seventy-two to ninety-six hours. The mudflats are a rich breeding ground for a tiny crustacean called *Corophium volutator.* There may be 10,000 to 40,000 of them in a square metre of sand. The birds engage in a feeding frenzy and double their weight in a week or two.

In 1988, the southern bight of the Minas Basin was designated by Canada and the Province of Nova Scotia as part of Canada's first shorebird reserve. It is part of an international program called the Western Hemisphere Shorebird Reserve Network, which was established for the purpose of protecting critical migration, staging, and wintering areas used by large concentrations of these birds. Other birds to be found here are the ruddy turnstone, black-bellied plover, semipalmated plover, short-billed dowitcher, and knot. These birds can also be seen at Kingsport, which is across the water and farther down the road on our tour.

Evangeline Beach is also a haven for swimmers. But unlike the predictable surf of other Maritime beaches, the mudflats and tides of the Minas Basin are a unique experience for the swimmer. Here is a local bather's advice on the matter, applicable to any of the basin beaches (Porter's Point, Blomidon Provincial Park Beach, Avonport, Kingsport, Medford, Houston's Beach):

The best time of day to swim is one hour before high tide because the returning water is relatively warm, having absorbed the heat soaked up by sun-exposed mudflats. When the tide turns there is half an hour before the wind changes and the water becomes colder.

Because of the considerable amount of silt that is picked up on the mudflats, the water is very murky. The color does not affect the water quality, but an underwater swimmer with goggles cannot see his hand in front of him. Feet and bodies get mucky, but the ground is firm. No need to panic—it's not quicksand.

When the water comes back, it has a long way to go over a flat plain in a relatively short time, so that it returns just about as fast as a swimmer can walk. If you find yourself on a sand dune or high patch, the water may suddenly seem to engulf you on all sides. Keep calm and be prepared to swim part of the way back. Swimming in with the tide is also part of the great fun of this unusual beach.

Consider the tides here. The water originates in the Gulf of Maine. The ocean tides may be two or three metres (seven to ten feet) as they originate at the continental shelf, but as they travel down the Bay of Fundy, through Minas Channel, and into the basin, tides measuring from 12 to 15 metres (40 to 50 feet) are not uncommon. Because of the length of this system the retreating water (every thirteen hours) meets the arrival of the next tidal energy pulse, thus causing a sloshing big wave. An excellent description of this phenomenon in *A Natural History of Kings County* (see Bibliography) uses the gentle rocking back and forth of a basin of water to explain how the exceptional waves are formed.

From Grand Pré National Historic Site drive back to Route 1 and cross at the intersection near the Evangeline Motel. (Hint: the snack bar has great peach and cherry pie in season made from fruit picked in the Sterling family orchards.) Continue straight to Wallbrook for a few blocks, to the Covenanter Church.

Built in 1811, the church is set in a canopy of mature maples, wrought-iron-fenced graves, and a carpet of periwinkles and English ivy. Looking at it with twentieth-century eyes (perhaps saturated by a chaos of coloured plastics) we are touched by the simple, beautifully proportioned eighteenth-century Georgian structure. Everything, including the tower, belfry, and steeple, the three-story pulpit, and the square-box pews, is handcrafted from wood. Above the pulpit is the original octagonal sounding board, which was used to project the reading (even to the servants upstairs in the gallery) and is said to work better than modern electronic equipment.

From June to December 20, services are held by the United Church and are designed to appeal to people of all faiths. Visitors are welcome to enjoy the special services, which include music and poetry.

Back at the corner, turn left on Route 1 to the town of Wolfville. Imagining a drive down lovely elm-lined Main Street 100 years ago is not difficult. Many of the beautiful stately homes have been preserved. The setting is lush vegetation, and the orchards and fields gradually yield to rhododendrons, rose bowers, and smoke bushes. Students of architecture will notice everything from simple Cape Cod style to grand Victorian and Queen Anne period buildings. For more detail, the tourist bureau in Willow Park has a pamphlet titled *Self-Guided Walking Tour of Wolfville Heritage Properties*, published by the Wolfville Heritage Advisory Committee. Wolfville is a culturally and commercially diverse university town (Acadia University). It supports a bookstore, art video store, many excellent restaurants and inns, and a wonderful coffee shop called the Coffee Merchant. The atmosphere in this shop is warm and unhurried. There is a bookshelf of eclectic magazines to browse through while enjoying coffees, teas, and desserts. In nice weather, customers sit outside at little tables and watch the hubbub of the street.

One block off Main Street toward the dyke land is Front Street, which used to be a commercial warehouse area along the train tracks. Since the demise of rail transportation, the area has been imaginatively rejuvenated. The old train station houses the public library; the apple warehouse has been subdivided into boutiques.

Across from the library is a curious freestanding brick chimney with a small, open-faced, wooden structure at its base. The chimney is all that is left of the Farmers Dairy building. In the mid 1970s, after the dairy stopped processing milk, the chimney became the summer nesting spot for hundreds of chimney swifts (*Chaetura pelagica*) after their long flight from Peru. When the building was scheduled for demolition, a local group called the Blomidon Naturalists Society rallied citizens to save the birds' home. They succeeded and have named it the Robie Tufts Nature Centre in honor of a local man whose infectious love of birds led him to serve as the chief migratory protection officer for the Maritimes for thirty years. He was the author of the classic *Birds of Nova Scotia*. Living a hardy ninety-five years, Tufts inspired generations of internationally known ornithologists and lay birdwatchers.

Sightings of the birds, who return to the chimney every evening, begin around the second week in May and continue until mid- to late August.

Every night, just before dusk, there is a swarming of humans next to the chimney. On a balmy night they arrive by foot. When the weather is clear but chilly, the parking lot fills with cars. Diners time their reservations at nearby restaurants to coincide with the setting of the sun and the arrival of the swifts.

At the first tweet of a bird, all eyes gaze skyward. At first there are a couple, then a few dozen, and soon the air is filled with hundreds of circling, swooping, and diving chimney swifts. Constantly moving in huge spirals, these birds have not set down on a branch or wire to rest all day. Then there is that magic still point when the birds form a funnel of flight and begin dropping, one by one, into the chimney. Others take several teasing tries, dive-bombing and recovering up into the air. But in a few minutes, all are safely anchored with their spiny quill feathers to the inside walls of their brick roost.

Back on Main Street, travel west on Route 1 through town to Greenwich corner, remembering always to keep the dyke land on the right. At this corner are two exceptional farm markets: Hennigar's Farm Market before the intersection, and Noggins Corner, a short distance past.

In June, the stands are covered with quarts of luscious strawberries, bedding plants, and rhubarb. As the summer progresses, there are raspberries and peas in the pod, and peaches and cream corn (by the bushel bag if you so desire). On a crisp fall day it feels like the Garden of Eden. Dozens of varieties of apples overflow wooden crates, fresh off the trees of the neighbouring orchards. Many are cherished historic varieties: Bough Sweet (an early apple), Bishop's Pippin (named after Nova Scotia's first Anglican Bishop), Gravenstein (ask Nova Scotians to identify their favorite apple and they always answer, Gravenstein!), and Cox's Orange (a spicy English variety with an orange blush and a tropical fragrance). There are also bushels of Clapp pears, Golden plums, Montmorency cherries, and Giant Atlantic squash that remind us of small Volkswagen Beetles. There are barrels of pure ambrosia—freshly squeezed apple cider.

At the corner turn down Route 41 toward Port Williams, Canning, and Kingsport. Travel across dyke land and the Cornwallis River to the village of Port Williams, once a bustling port that exported barrels of apples to Great Britain. Continue through the village, turning right at the yellow flashing light toward Starrs Point.

We follow this road for a few miles until the landscape and view open up. Blomidon is on the left. Follow the signs to Prescott House at Starrs Point.

Along the way are pick-your-own farms selling apples, highbush blueberries, and raspberries. Never is fruit so fresh and fragrant as when we pick it ourselves, and it is less expensive than in the stores, too. Nova Scotians from all parts of the province make annual pilgrimages to the valley for these apples and berries.

Prescott House, part of the Nova Scotia Museum complex, is a grand Georgian-style home. Built by Charles Ramage Prescott, who is credited with having brought the Gravenstein apple to the Annapolis Valley, the house was restored by his granddaughter, Mary Prescott. When she took on the task in the 1930s, the house was in a sad state. Animals had been stabled in it and farm workers had ripped up the hardwood floors for kindling (it's hard to believe, looking at it today.) The gardens and grounds are of particular historic interest.

From here the road twists and turns through barnyards and orchards of extraordinary pastoral beauty. Some of the roads have no signs, but keep in mind that we are always

going in the direction of Blomidon. We follow the path closest
to the basin wherever possible.

Loop around Starrs Point and, at a man-made pond, turn
right, just past the Norland Farm (the sign says "Lower
Canard 2 km and the Wellington Dyke").

Brownish salt marsh growing next to green dyke land
gives us some idea of what this land looked like when it was
all wild marsh. In summer the great blue herons are silent,
aloof observers on stilts. It is a thrill to see them take flight. In
winter bald eagles are common in this area, and bus tours
come from miles around to see them. Just ahead is a "running
dyke," so called because it runs alongside the water. The
inner protected western side is about six metres (twenty feet)
lower than the exposed basin side.

A sign at the Wellington Dyke states, "Protecting 3030
acres. First protected 1812. Maintained by the Nova Scotia
Dept. of Agriculture and Marketing." Underneath this dyke is
the aboiteau, a culvertlike device, used to discharge fresh
water that builds up behind the dyke. The aboiteau (originally
constructed of hollowed logs and now of sawn timber) has a
hinged one-way door that allows fresh water out, at low tide,
while restricting the entrance of seawater at high tide. For
more information refer to an excellent book called *Maritime
Dykelands: The 350-Year Struggle* (see Bibliography).

Turn right toward Lower Canard and drive through gentle farmland and huge expanses of sky where grand old
homes framed by ancient elm trees point to past prosperity.

There is an unmarked left turn at the next road (going
straight we will end up at Porter's Point, a dead end). Follow
this road through the unclaimed salt marsh and cross over the
Habitant River to a stop sign and, straight ahead, a gambrel-
roofed house (said to have been transported by barge from
New England).

Turn right at the corner toward Kingsport, travelling past the "Welcome to Kingsport" sign. Turn left at Longspell Road, then left again on Jackson Barkhouse Road and head straight toward Blomidon, through potato and vegetable fields. At this higher elevation, the soil is reddish and very different from the dyke soil. During plowing, the fields are spotted with gluttonous seagulls, feasting on worms and grubs. Turn left at the stop sign at Weaver Road, and then turn right, continuing down Jackson Barkhouse Road.

At the North Medford Road, continue straight and descend into the valley of the Pereaux River. The extraordinary view of contrasting perspectives at the base of the mountain must be the residents' best-kept secret. The road is sheltered on one side by a huge snakelike dyke as it winds its way into the river valley.

At the stop sign turn right toward Lower Blomidon. At Delhaven is a government wharf, a gorgeous view of Paddy's Island, and the mudflats.

Like a decorative ribbon border, the road keeps a safe distance, but faithfully edges the erratic meandering of the highly eroded shoreline. The view out to the basin broadens with each mile. And then, there, amidst green hills and fields—majestically placed almost within our grasp—is Blomidon itself. The road dips into a gully and Blomidon's cape whimsically plays a game of hide-and-seek with us, sinking down and then up as our car ventures to the next rise.

Thanks to the provincial parks system, Blomidon's wooded mountainside and 180-metre (600-foot) cliffs are not a formidable mystery to man but an accessible friend.

At the entrance to Blomidon Provincial Park is a picnic area with access to the beach. (Farther up the hill are camping facilities.) Borden Brook, which once supported a sawmill, pours off the mountain heights and drops abruptly to the beach below. Carved out of the cliff, for our respite, is a civilized patch of grass, some picnic tables, and a few pit toilets.

It's only twenty-five stairs down to the beach, where we can touch the cliffs that we eyed from far across the water at Grand Pré. As they crumble in our hands it is easy to see where the silted mudflats have originated. While we're here, we enjoy the shorebirds, tide pools, and marine plants and animals.

A word of caution: remember that the tides here are amongst the highest in the world. They rise and fall twice a day, and the funnelling effect on the Minas Basin causes them to have a range of 12 metres (40 feet). What this means is that as we stand in one spot, on bare sand, the water can rise up to our armpits in twenty minutes.

After leaving the park, double back and turn right on the Lookoff Road. Climb the gravel road that leads up the bed of Mill Creek to the farmland above. Turn left at the top and travel 5 kilometres (3 miles) of nondescript road. At the opening in the trees, it will become apparent why we have come here.

Standing at the top of it all, we look down from the place to which we have looked up all day. Lingering at the railing of the lookoff, hot air rises up from the valley and an eagle, wings spread, soars on the updraft. The humming wind resonates through the trees. And below is a complex quilt of hues. It is absolutely astonishing to consider exactly how many shades there are of green and gold and blue.

Follow the road down the mountain, through Canning, and back to the main road.

In the Area

Beveridge Arts Centre, Acadia University (Wolfville): 902-542-2201

Box of Delights Bookstore (Wolfville): 902-542-9511

The Coffee Merchant (Wolfville): 902-542-4315

Evangeline Motel and Snack Bar (Grand Pré): 902-542-2703

Noggins Corner Farm (Greenwich): 902-542-1791

Grand Pré National Historic Site (Grand Pré): 902-542-3631

Hennigar's Farm Market (Greenwich): 902-542-3503

Prescott House, Nova Scotia Museum (Starrs Point): 902-542-3984

Wolfville Heritage Advisory Committee (Wolfville Town Hall): 902-542-5767

Wolfville Tourist Bureau (Wolfville): 902-542-7000

9 ~

Rocky Peninsulas:

Yarmouth County

From Yarmouth: Take Main Street south. The road goes for 65 kilometres (40 miles) from Yarmouth to Chebogue Point, Tusket, and West Pubnico. Travel time without stops: 1.5 hours.

Highlights: *Chebogue Point, Town Point Cemetery, the Tusket Islands, Argyle Township Court House and Gaol, Sluice Point, Ste. Anne du Ruisseau, Rocco Point, the Argyles, the barrens, West Pubnico, D'Eon's Bakery.*

Leaving downtown Yarmouth, we follow Main Street south as it heads out along Yarmouth Sound. The road climbs high above the sea. The view can be expansive or shrouded in fog. This harbour is home to the large ferries, which cruise in from Portland and Bar Harbor, Maine, and also tiny Cape Island fishing boats, which steam into port, swarmed by eager seagulls. The land close at hand is called the "Rum Nubble." (We'd love to know how it got its name.) The land afar is Cape Forchu.

A few miles down the road is Kelly's Cove. In spite of the sparse vegetation and an overgenerous supply of boulders (where trees would have been preferable), life has gone on here for generations. Modest homes are scattered over the terrain and a testimony to the tenacity of the early settlers lies in the ably crafted stone walls that snake and grid the hills. We can, now, only just imagine the raggle-taggle sheep and cows that noisily inhabited these stony compounds when life was lived at the bare bones of subsistence.

Proceed on to Rockville and turn right at Rockville United Baptist Church toward Chebogue Point. This is a 5-kilometre

Yarmouth Light and Harbour from Kelly's Cove

(3-mile) dead-end road, but it is well worth the doubling back. We stop at the corner to contemplate the view—the blue of the Chebogue River and the hazy islands beyond. The word Chebogue comes from two Mi'kmaq words: *che*, meaning "great" and *poug*, meaning "still water." Our road follows the banks of this great, aptly named estuary.

More of the river comes into view as we drive down the rolling peninsula, past cows and gardens. In summer, residents grow squash and cucumbers right next to the road. At the end, however, vegetation is sparse. On a small knoll, a half dozen 30-metre-high (100-foot-high) futuristic radio towers and a complex of wire rigging witness the view out to the Gulf of Maine and beyond.

On the ground there is a fantastic view of the spits, reefs, and headlands (including Linnys Head, Pompees Head, and Crawleys Head). We don't need a geology degree to visualize what goes on here when the crashing surf and the howling wind meet the glacial gravel till of this shore. The headlands are high and abrupt. The tapered reefs look like huge sea slugs.

In the distance are the Tusket Islands. Their names tantalize the imagination. We want to know more about them: Murder, Candlebox, Tarpaulin, Turpentine, Inner Spectacle, and Little Half Bald Islands. Were they named on the whim of the surveyor general who mapped the area, or does each island have an intriguing story to tell? Do the folks at the local store know their secrets?

On the drive back to the corner, the wildflowers surround us. The swallows and killdeers swoop in front of the car and the cows that graze in the fields nod as we pass.

At the corner turn right and travel for a mile to the Chebogue United Church of Canada, where a sign reads "Town Point—No Exit." Turn down this road to the Town Point Cemetery, bounded by the Chebogue River on one side and a "dry stone wall" on the other. It is *dry* because the stones fit together with such precision that they have remained in place for a century or more without the benefit of a smattering of mortar.

On the stone wall a plaque reads: "This tablet commemorates the landing of the first English speaking settlers near this spot on June 9, 1761." It was placed here by the Yarmouth County Historical Society in 1956.

For travellers who've never considered a cemetery to be an interesting place to explore, this is a good one to start at. Cherished for generations, it is a Provincially Registered Heritage Property and features one of the most peaceful landscapes in Nova Scotia.

Etched into stone is one man's testimony to the beauty of this plot on the banks of the Chebogue River. Donald Browning Prentice was born in Providence, Rhode Island, in November 23, 1907, and died there on March 8, 1984, but he was laid to rest here. This grave tells a poignant story of the emotional bond between Nova Scotians and "the Boston States." His tombstone reads:

He loved this spot
With its landscapes and seascapes
The liquid clarity of its light and its color
all soft and caressing
making a unity of earth and sea and sky.

The graves are set into terraces that descend down to the gently moving estuary below. The stones tell the stories of men lost at sea and whole families wiped out by disease. Dozens of horse chestnut trees form a candelabrum of blooms in spring and a canopy of shaded greens in summer. In winter their empty wood frames shelter the graves.

In the middle of the grey tombstones splashed with yellow lichen is a sculpted marble lady reclining on a sheaf of wheat. This is the grave of Margaret McNaught Webster, mother of ten, who died on August 27, 1864, at the age of forty-nine. She was the wife of Dr. Frederick Augustus Webster, the first doctor to practise in the town of Yarmouth. Apparently while studying medicine in Scotland, he went for a stroll in the country and came upon Margaret, a young lass, asleep on a sheaf of wheat.

After his wife died Dr. Webster had this image of his love, as he had first encountered her, carved into pure white Italian marble by the sculptor S. F. Raymond. Margaret Webster's funeral was held in Yarmouth and her coffin was taken by boat, accompanied by a procession of rowboats, around Chebogue Point and up the channel of the river for her final rest.

There is a quarried stone chapel with a comfortable bench in front. From here we can see beyond the sedentary chestnuts and grave markers. The background is a flurry of activity at the government wharf. Fishing boats are loading and unloading, trucks are coming and going. Behind this is the river channel and wooded Clements Island. We can see why Donald Browning Prentice loved this spot.

Now proceed back to the corner and on to Central Chebogue. This side of the peninsula (unlike the Kelly's Cove area) is not only protected from prevailing Atlantic gales, but also has been blessed by the retreating glaciers with an essential for farming—soil. The drive is pleasant, through green farmland dotted with trees, cows, greenhouses, and even a dairy.

At Arcadia the back-road choices for travellers dramatically increase with the lay of the land. While we will stick primarily to Route 3, other roads diverge like the roots of a tree. It is possible to find your own secret harbour, but it'll likely be at the conclusion of a dead-end road. Plan for the turn-back time.

This landscape includes hundreds of narrow fingers of rock separated by briny inlets. At the end of the last Ice Age the melting glaciers caused the sea to rise and the tips of the peninsula fingers were separated, forming islands.

This area was called *Papkoktek* by the Mi'kmaq. They spent their winters inland, hunting, and in the spring they paddled down the interconnected streams and lakes to spend their summers by the sea. Their name means "always running down," and it well describes the landscape.

The Europeans who settled this land arrived in sailing ships. Their livelihood, indeed their basic survival, depended on fish. They settled close to where they first landed. Scattered at the edge of the stony rock peninsulas, some of which are 50 kilometres (30 miles) or more long, are houses aplenty and silver grey outbuildings. The roads were built much later, on the high ground, through the centre of each finger. There are dozens of back roads to choose from. But it's important to get off the road and down to the water. From this perspective, the shoreline, with its drowned fjords and hardwood-covered islands is extraordinary. A note to back-road adventurers: please check tires for air pressure and have a functional spare. It is important to take drinking water and something to eat. A pair of rubber boots or hiking boots is essential for exploring the shore and, because of the remarkable difference between the inland and the offshore climate (what a difference a little fog and a sea wind can make), be sure to pack a jacket. This is not meant to discourage, but only to make the trip more comfortable. There's nothing like finding a secluded rubble beach, nesting down into the sun-warmed palm of a giant granite form, and feeling like the only soul on earth. But this is possible only with the proper footwear—sandals won't get us there.

Follow Route 3 to Tusket, a good place to get out of the car and have a stretch. At the head of the river mouth is a tiny picnic park with a lovely view.

Tusket was founded by New Englanders in 1761. Dutch Loyalists followed in 1784, making it the largest Dutch settlement in the province. The interior of old St. Stephen's Church reflects the austere "reformed" background of its founders.

There is a sharp turn at the corner and an antique store called The Hanging Oak. The proprietors can dispense directions to their namesake, a gnarled and ancient tree, which is the subject of some historical controversy.

The Argyle Township Court House and Gaol (Ancien Palais de Justice) is located in the centre of Tusket. It is the oldest standing courthouse in Canada and was actively used from 1805 until 1976. The courtroom and cells are open to the public during the summer months. At the rear of the building, archives and a research library for historical and genealogical research are open year-round.

For a peninsula diversion take the road behind Tusket to Hubbard's Point, Amirault's Hill, Sluice Point, and Surette's and Morris Islands. Settled by French Acadian pioneers who returned to this area after exile to New England in the 1770s, the French road signs here are an indication of how the French culture still thrives.

A large salt marsh separates Hubbard's Point from Amirault's Hill. Posts embedded in the marsh are support platforms, called staddles, for drying marsh hay. This traditional harvest method has been employed for hundreds of years, starting with the Acadians who brought dyke-making technology from France. One of the first tasks of pioneers was to clear the land for farming. Considering the primitive hand tools available at that time, dyking the sea seemed an easier task than cutting down the virgin timber stands to make fields.

We travel through Sluice Point to the Indian Sluice, a channel of water that separates the mainland from Surette's Island. The power of the converging tides at this point is staggering. The iron bridge crossing the narrow channel was built in 1909 and was considered a great engineering feat at the time. It was built upriver and floated into place on the rushing tide.

In the churchyard on Surette's Island is a famous grave. The tombstone of Marie Babin Surette says that she died in 1862 at the age of 110 and that she was the last survivor of all the Acadian deportees who returned to Nova Scotia.

A mile past the Indian Sluice bridge is another bridge to Morris Island (Ile à Morris) and a grand view of the bay. Travellers may wish to explore the islands further or follow us as we retrace our steps back to Tusket and Route 3.

We travel through a few kilometres of woods to a bridge where an expansive marsh drains Eel Lake at Ste. Anne du Ruisseau. Nearby is a magnificent white and black-trimmed wooden structure, Ste. Anne's Church. This Catholic parish is the oldest in the region, having been established in 1799. The original building was destroyed by fire in 1890 and replaced by the present church in 1902. Guided tours are given throughout the summer months.

Next to the church is a pretty side road to Rocco Point. At the end of the road is a small wharf on a body of water called the Little Sluice. In 1784 Pierre Mius built a log-cabin chapel here. It was the first church to be built in southwestern Nova Scotia after the return of the Acadians following the expulsion. Priest Abbé Jean Mande Sigogne, exiled from France during the French Revolution, sailed into this harbour on a fishing schooner in 1799. He built a church, which is the spiritual predecessor of the current Ste. Anne's.

Double back to Route 3. The highway straddles the centre of another finger of land, and the water view can be enjoyed on both sides of the road.

There's a rest stop at Glenwood Provincial Park, at the junction of Route 103 and Route 3. There are picnic tables under the shade of hardwood trees and a view of Ricker's Lake.

At exit 32A, Route 3 briefly joins Route 103 to cross the Argyle River. This can be a bit confusing, so be sure to turn left after the bridge and head back onto Route 3 toward Argyle Head.

The road follows the meandering Argyle River as it expands into Argyle Sound. The Argyles were named by Capt. Ranald McKinnon after his home in Scotland. After the expulsion of the Acadians, he was granted 800 hectares (2,000 acres) in the area. Other settlers were mostly New Englanders who arrived in the 1760s. The Argyle Historic Church in Argyle, a Municipal and Provincial Historic Property, has background material on early settlement.

On this stretch of highway, the water side of the road tends to rivet our attention. On the other side of the road we notice expanses of land carpeted with moss and devoid of trees and bushes. These bogs are fascinating places in their own right. They can be found all over the region, thriving anywhere plant nutrients are scarce and water is abundant.

Yarmouth County has many areas like this—acres of rock basins that collect rainwater and have little soil to attract other plant forms. The chief inhabitant of the bog is sphagnum or "peat moss." These plants are modest in their needs, requiring only air, water, and light. Their leaves are only one cell thick, but soak up forty times their weight in water, forming a huge floating sponge that chokes out competition.

Above the bogs are the dry, rocky barrens, home of wild blueberries. At the turn of the century blueberries were an important cash crop in the local economy. Pickers would spend weeks in the barrens. The berries were hauled out with oxen, and the cart tracks down to the wharves in Yarmouth were purported to have been stained blue by crushed berries. The high-quality berries (with the frosty "bloom" still intact) were famous in Boston. Largely because of the high labor costs, fresh, locally picked blueberries are hard to find in the stores today. However this doesn't mean that the berries aren't still around. Sometimes enterprising children flog quarts of berries from a card table in their driveway.

Starting around August 15, blueberries grow on the rocky road allowances. It's a satisfying chore to stop and pick enough for lunch.

As the road climbs, we soak in the last of Argyle Sound and the silver, silhouetted islands glistening in the distance. The road toward the Pubnicos veers inland for a few kilometres. Turn left at the corner where a big fieldstone cairn honours Sieur Phillipe d'Entremont, who first settled in this area in 1651.

Let's get our Pubnicos straight: there's Pubnico, Upper West Pubnico, West Pubnico, Middle West Pubnico, and Lower West Pubnico. And that's only on the west side of Pubnico Harbour. But don't be intimidated—a trip to this peninsula is worth it, if only for the cake doughnuts at D'Eon's Bakery.

West Pubnico (and surrounds) is a quiet, tidy, close-knit, and very proudly Acadian community. The telephone book reads like the list of the original settlers: two whole pages of d'Entremonts, many Amiraults, D'Eons, Surettes, Comeaus, and Belliveaus.

It is a peninsula, like much of the rest of this drive, so we explore the back roads here. Cruising through, we get a feel for the place by reading the signs: Bibliothèque de Public, Banque Royal, Vernon D'Eon Lobster Plugs Ltd., Amirault—concrete ballast, D'Eon Fish Market, D'Eon's Bakery. The welcome sign reads, "Bienvenue West Pubnico Ouest."

119

The view of Pubnico Harbour is gentle. Following the water for a few miles down the peninsula, we sense the intensity of the relationship between the people who live here and the sea. This is a community of fishermen and boatbuilders.

The bakery in Upper West is a simple, clean, white building but inside it is a tapestry of fragrance. The aroma of cinnamon buns and spicy molasses drops, jam cookies, and brownies fills the air day and night. Why not get a dozen cookies for the road? They sell rappie pie, a traditional Acadian potato casserole, and for those who want to make it at home, rappie pie mix.

The Musée Acadien, opposite the fire station in West Pubnico, was an Acadian home built in 1864. It features household items, books, pictures, maps, and the original land grants from the late 1700s. This museum tells the story of the families who came from France in 1651 with Charles de la Tour, were violently expelled in "Le Grand Derangement" of 1755, and had the tenacity to return and pick up the pieces of their lives. (It is open June 15 to Labour Day.)

If there has been any theme to this drive it has been that Pubnico, like so many other communities along this rocky shore, has struggled but managed to survive in an extraordinarily beautiful and challenging environment. This ends our tour but you may want to explore the west side of Pubnico Harbour. Return on Route 335 to Route 103, where you can continue your coast journey, or take the fast track to Halifax or Yarmouth.

In the Area

Argyle Township Court House and Gaol (Tusket):
  902-648-0367

D'Eon's Bakery (Upper West Pubnico): 902-762-2312

The Hanging Oak (Tusket): 902-648-2668

Saint Anne's Church Rectory (Ste. Anne du Ruisseau): 902-648-2315

Yarmouth County Tourist Association (Yarmouth): 902-742-5355

10 ~
Beaches of Lunenburg County

From Halifax: Take Route 103 west for 125 kilometres (75 miles) to exit 17 to East Port Medway, Voglers Cove, and Cherry Hill.

From Yarmouth: Take Route 103 east for 165 kilometres (100 miles) to exit 17. The road follows the Atlantic shore for 40 kilometres (25 miles) to LaHave. Travel time without stops: one hour.

Highlights: *Cherry Hill Beach, piping plovers, Broad Cove, First Settler's Cemetery, Petite Rivière, Bargain Bob's, Macleod's Canteen, Green Bay, Rissers Beach, Crescent Beach, LaHave Islands, LaHave River, Foreign Protestants, LaHave Bakery and ferry.*

After the big highway, it's a relief to get onto this smaller woodsy road, but be prepared for a good 7-kilometre (4-mile) drive before we get to the shore. Just over the Lunenburg County line is the Voglers Cove sign and there, as compact as a child's shoebox diorama—framed by trees—is a peek at Medway Harbour, all green and blue, islands and sea, and a taste of more to come.

The village of Voglers Cove is a tiny grouping of gothic houses clustered around a sheltered inlet called Conrad Cove. Voglers Brook trickles into the cove at the side of the road as we pass through. If there ever was such a thing as the old

122

swimming hole, this is it. On a balmy day we are tempted to join the local children, basking on rocks and splashing up to their elbows in brook water.

The road from here to Cherry Hill Beach will give us a real feel for Lunenburg County. The road is carefully incised into the smooth, cultivated hillside. We see down and away for miles: a quilt of woods and tiny farms, voluminous sky and glistening blue patches of sea. The mystery of what is up and over that next hill lures us on.

Coming up a few miles past Voglers Cove is one of the most raw and unpredictable, yet magical, beaches on the South Shore of Nova Scotia—Conrad Beach on Hell Bay, but everyone calls it Cherry Hill Beach. The spruce woods on the rough drive to the beach seem enchanted. The wide, gnarled trunks are studded with branches, half dead. Those living are weighted down with a drapery of old man's-beard moss. This is what trees have to do to survive in a land of relentless wind and salt and fog.

We park behind the barrier of surf-smoothed cobbles that cradles the sand of the beach while sheltering the lagoon behind. Barely out of the car, even before we have seen the beach, our senses are overwhelmed. We are whipped by that pungent raw iodine smell of the North Atlantic. And there is the roar of air trapped in rumbling rocks, the swash and backwash of the waves, and the bursting bubbles of the frothy suds. Crossing through a path in the dune, we finally see the source of all this sound and smell—the beach.

Cherry Hill Beach is never the same, and never what we expect. In spring the skyscape may be mauve with a palpable metallic freshness to the air. Turning off the highway on a glorious summer day, we may be confronted by a cold, clammy wall of fog. The sharp drop in temperature can be a shock or a relief on an unbearably muggy day. After an August hurricane or winter storm has raked the ocean bottom, we find ourselves picking our way across a thigh-deep twisted mat. Three-metre-long (ten-foot-long) strands of kelp, bubble-bladdered rockweed, and dead man's finger sponges have all washed up.

What we remember, though, are those precious summer days when an aquamarine surf and sky come together to invite bathers to renew themselves in the great heartbeat of the waves.

Cherry Hill Beach is the nesting ground of the piping plover, which since 1985 has been on the list of endangered Canadian species compiled by the Committee on the Status of Endangered Wildlife in Canada. Because this bird nests right in the sand (above high tide), cradling its eggs only with wisps of eelgrass and shell shards, it has been threatened by human activity. Eggs are most at risk in May and June, and signs posted at the entrance to the beach entreat visitors to walk close to the tide line and to keep dogs leashed. Piping plovers are a delight for those of us lucky enough to see them. To protect their nests from intruders they approach us at a distance, taking wide circles, streaking in short sprints in an almost comical fashion. With a sixth sense for the ebb and flow, they dodge the waves while grabbing a bite to eat like little busybodies on roller blades.

A few miles past Cherry Hill Beach, the road takes an abrupt turn. For an insight into small-scale inshore fishing, a postcard-perfect snapshot, or a place to set up an easel for the day, diverge from the pavement and go straight down the Little Harbour Wharf Road. The steep gravel leads to a finger of water in the greywacke just large enough to sustain a wharf and a handful of wooden boats painted the brilliant yellows and reds of a Crayola box. There are fish sheds weathered silver grey and a collage of buoys and lobster pots, starfish and periwinkles. In lobster season (November to May) this is a busy place. The fishermen are not necessarily in the mood for a leisurely chat, but they are in the mood to sell us lobster.

Lobstermen

Just down the road, where a sign announces the outer limits of Broad Cove, is a spot where so many elements of beauty come together that it couldn't have been orchestrated by the human hand. Not many people know by name Arties Pond and Arties Cove, as they are shown on a detailed topographic map. This is certainly not a tourist-designated lookoff. But so many people have idled onto the shoulder of the road, and turned off the engine to listen to the surf, that the gravel has naturally spread out like a welcome mat. What makes this place so special? It's true that the pond in summer is an explosion of lily pad blossoms. And the view out to sea is as far as the imagination will allow. But our guess is that it has something to do with the perspective of the human eye: the juxtaposition of images, which include the rubble beach, which seems to flow onto the road, the rounded curve of the cultivated hill, and the green bell buoy, bobbing on the wild sea. It is a point of view between water and water that makes us feel like privileged land animals resting safely, albeit briefly, between two water spirits.

A bit farther down the road at the top of the hill is one of the most spectacular vistas on the South Shore—a panoramic view of the village of Broad Cove and out to sea as far as the LaHave Islands (which we visit later).

At the bottom of the hill is the Broad Cove Community Hall, famous for its ham-and-potato-scallop suppers in summer and its dances in winter; so watch for signs (or check the tourist bureau or local paper for dates). Just past the hall, turn down Beach Road where a breakwater protects a tiny sand beach.

Behind the beach is the First Settler's Cemetery. The names on the tombstones are those of German souls who settled Lunenburg County in the 1800s and earlier: Wamboldt, Wentzell, Vogler, Teel, Borgel, Morash, and Herman. These same names are painted on the mail boxes planted along the strip of highway. Many of the wooden framed houses that sheltered these buried pioneers are still standing, although evolved: clapboard has been overlaid with pine shingles or perhaps a coating of vinyl. Fortunately there are many houses along this shore where the touch of the craftsman before the days of electrical tools is still in evidence: the bubbles in the blown-glass panes, the hand-turned gingerbread in the doorways.

The houses are perched askew on the shore. Their placement is a puzzle to modern travellers, but their front doors were built to welcome returning sailors in the days when overland travel was a tiresome, slow business on foot or horse over treacherous paths.

The cemetery tells the story of a hard life in seaside communities before the coming of paved roads and telephones with inscriptions like "In memory of Joseph F., son of Joseph and Mary M. Smith, who fell from the main boom of the schooner *J. B. Huey* off White Head and was drowned, January 24, 1865, aged 22 years."

Behind the beach is the trail to Beartrap Cove, which is the start of the old road to Green Bay, now in disrepair and accessible only to those on foot, horse, or mountain bike. It's a splendid hike that faithfully follows the shoreline for 13 kilometres (8 miles). After three hours we end up in Green Bay, where we have definitely earned our dinner at Macleod's Canteen. We cleverly have asked a friend to drive the car around to pick us up. Watch the tides and have proper walking shoes, which are best on the cobble and sand walking surfaces.

For those of us not able to walk the shore, the road takes an unfortunate dip inland for about 12 kilometres (7 miles). We zoom on to scenic Petite Rivière, just ahead. Spying cars parked by the side of the road with their occupants curiously crouched in the ditch, we screech to a stop. In August they are picking blueberries; in October, it's cranberries. In December, when we think that Mother Nature is fast asleep, the residents are still parked off to the side of the road, clipping armloads of a red-berried shrub commonly known as Nova Scotia holly for their outdoor Christmas bouquets.

The road wends its way down into the valley to a sign that reads "Petite Rivière Welcomes You, founded 1632." This lovely village clustered around the rushing river is a curious mixture of homes and commercial enterprises. It is a good place to stretch legs and poke around. At the corner where an iron bridge spans the river is the Covey Island Boatworks. A peek inside the old glass storefront window reveals a collection of shackles, bolts and turnbuckles, nautical charts, brass and chrome this and that. Last year this company built the *Tree of Life*, a wooden yacht that was named one of the ten best boats in the world by *Yachting* magazine.

Across the street is a convenience store complete with a gas pump. On the opposite corner is an antique store. Just up the road is the volunteer fire department (watch for a sign for community suppers), a bed and breakfast, and Bargain Bob's Used Clothing, which is a secondhand Gap and L. L. Bean at rock-bottom prices. As a break from rifling through bins of clothes cast off by wealthy New Englanders, customers have only to glance up and look out the windows of the shop at the extraordinary Petite River flowing by.

A little side road at the corner leads to Green Bay and Macleod's Canteen (open Victoria Day to Labour Day). We follow the estuary on the left out to sea. Rissers Beach is across the river, partially hidden by clumps of trees. On the right, emerald pastures dotted with cows carpet the steep slopes and remind us that much of rural Lunenburg County is farmland. Sperry's Beach, just past the Odd Fellows' Hall, is the residents' choice swimming spot.

The tiny summer community of Green Bay has the feel of old-fashioned cottage country of the 1920s. The twisty paved road follows the dips and turns of the shoreline. The cottages have manicured lawns, fieldstone fireplaces, and names like Polliwog, Kaermano Kamp, and Seawind.

On a warm summer evening Macleod's Canteen serves a zillion flavors of ice cream through its front sliding window. Inside the specialty is lobster chowder and freshly baked scones. The dress is simple: sandy bare feet and sweatshirt-covered bathing suits are the norm. The blueberry shortcake, made with a whipped cream smothered biscuit, is well worth a 17-kilometre (10-mile) diversion.

This business was started in 1929 by Malcolm and Rhoda Macleod, who sold homemade ice cream under a tarp to supplement their Depression income. It is now managed by their daughter Miriam MacIntosh and her family. They also rent modest cabins back in the woods with names such as Jalna and Idyll Wild.

To cut our tour short, there's a scenic way back to the fast road (Route 103). Follow the road that chases alongside the Petite Rivière through Crousetown and Italy Cross.

Back in Petite Rivière and on Route 331, cross the bridge to the east side of the river and up and around the scenic bend to Rissers Beach Provincial Park.

Rissers Beach is for teenagers who need other teenagers and french fries with their surf. The beach is absolutely spectacular and will be enjoyed as well by adults who wish to tag along. There's limited camping at the provincial park and a guided tour through the salt marsh. The parking lot is across the road, and bathers walk through the underground culvert to get to the sand.

A few miles down the road is Crescent Beach. This is one of the few beaches where vehicular traffic is allowed. Instead of driving right across, however, we prefer to park the car at the entrance, to step out on the sand to get a sense of the lay of the land. We stand on a crescent-shaped bar of hard-packed white sand embellished by a ruffle of waves. Within a 360-degree sweep of the water and land we note the shape and position of the LaHave Islands. Soon we will have our perspective turned all around. The water is blue azure and calm in summer but in the winter this body of angry, frothy, mint-coloured brine is accurately named Green Bay.

This beach is a geological rarity: a tombolo or sand bar that joins the mainland with an island. It's a strange feeling to drive across the beach that stretches for over 1.6 kilometres (1 mile) to George Island, the first in the archipelago of islands.

When the glaciers last tore through here over 10,000 years ago, they left behind tons of loose sand and gravel. Crescent Beach is nature's way of sorting through all the debris. While the outside headlands are continually attacked by the waves and pummelled into steep cliffs, the gentle lee sides of the islands benefit with daily contributions of the fine quartzite that makes up this spectacular moon-shaped beach.

As we travel this unusual land bridge, we notice the calm backwater known as Dublin Bay. Once we are on terra firma, the interconnected roads and bridges will allow us to explore George, Bush, Jenkins, and Bell Islands. The narrow, woodsy paths end at 150-year-old Cape Cod-style homes, summer cottages, and modern bungalows. Sprinkled amongst the rocks are fishermen's wharves, turquoise boat hulls, fluorescent buoys, and silver grey wood. Each gravelly little drive gives a different spin on the view. As we stand at the edge of Bell Island and stare across the Wolfe Gut, over Tumblin Island, Crooked Channel, and George Island, we can see back to where we first laid eyes on this spot.

On the mainland, turn right toward the LaHave River. The road goes inland for a few miles and then the view opens up again at Dublin Shore. A unique group of houses, walls, and a bridge built with rounded beach stones lines the area between the road and the shore. A small lane at the edge of a lily pond leads up to the small workshop that houses New Dublin Water Craft. This shop specializes in small, traditional wooden boats: canoes and South Shore dories.

Dublin Shore is at the mouth of the LaHave River, and it is here that the rugged, austere coast gradually transforms into the softer pastoral landscape of LaHave. It is easy to imagine how the seventeenth-century French settlers felt welcomed by this lush and tranquil harbour after spending weeks aboard creaky wooden ships. Look for the sign at Fort Point where the French landed under Isaac de Razilly, the first governor of New France who built Fort Sainte-Marie-de-Grace on this site in 1632. Fort Point features a museum and an exceptionally fine view of the river mouth.

In an enthusiastic letter home de Razilly described a veritable paradise: a sea "paved" with fish such as salmon and turbot, woods with lumber for an infinite number of boats, and enough mussels to feed all of Europe. Historical documents such this seem tinged with sad irony. While these resources exist to this day, and form a good part of the economic activity of the area, their finite nature is now well recognized.

The largest wave of settlement to LaHave came when the British imported thousands of "Foreign Protestants" from Germany, Switzerland, and France. They were settled in the town of Lunenburg but were also given farm lots that extended as far as the LaHave and Petite Rivière areas. The lists of immigrant passengers are available in the Public Archives in Halifax and a fascinating study can be made of the evolution of family names (i.e., Rotenhauser to Rhodenizer, Wheyle to Wile, Suderusch to Suderick, Bubikauffer to Publicover, Weinacht to Whynot, Schwinhiemer to Swinamer).

Just up the river from Fort Point is the tiny community of LaHave, where we take a cable ferry across the river for fifty cents—a very good price for a boat ride. The ferry runs on the hour and holds about ten cars. At the height of the tourist season, it doesn't hurt to get there a little early.

A stop by the LaHave Bakery, just down from the ferry, is a must. The store originally housed an outfitting company that sold provisions to the salt bankers that filled the harbour in the great days of sail. The building is being renovated to house a number of small businesses, including the bakery.

The original furnishings, including curved glass display cases, pressed metal ceilings, wooden walls, and shelving, are worth seeing for their historical value alone.

At the bakery the yeasty aroma of baking bread and the smell of freshly brewed coffee will also tantalize the visitor. At the very least we try to pick up a few brownies (with rich, dark, gooey insides) to relish on the boat. In summer the owners of the bakery also outfit yachts and offer nature cruises around the river and islands.

The fresh breeze off the centre of the river is a delightful relief on a hot summer's evening. The saucy, noisy seagulls swirl and dive-bomb. Ospreys hover, then drop, suddenly, like stones into the drink. The black shadows hanging off the harbour buoys—the cormorants—are more aloof. They are content with the serious business of drying their wings. The trip does not seem long enough.

Once on dry land turn left and follow Route 332 up to Bridgewater and then to the main highway, Route 103. For more of Lunenburg County, turn right and carry on to Rose Bay, Lunenburg, Mahone Bay, and any of the wonderful crossroads between.

In the Area

Bargain Bob's New and Used Clothing (Petite Rivière):
902-688-2295

Covey Island Boat Works Ltd. (Petite Rivière):
902-688-2843

LaHave Bakery and Outfitters (LaHave):
902-688-2908

LaHave Ferry information (LaHave): 902-688-2443

Macleod's Cottages and Canteen (Green Bay): 902-688-2212,
902-668-2866

New Dublin Water Craft (Dublin Shore): 902-688-2903

Nova Scotia Department of Natural Resources (for information on parks, Rissers Beach): 902-688-2010, 902-688-2034, 902-688-2782

South Shore Tourism Association (Mahone Bay): 902-624-6466

11 ~

Harbour Villages of the Eastern Shore

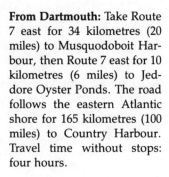

From Dartmouth: Take Route 7 east for 34 kilometres (20 miles) to Musquodoboit Harbour, then Route 7 east for 10 kilometres (6 miles) to Jeddore Oyster Ponds. The road follows the eastern Atlantic shore for 165 kilometres (100 miles) to Country Harbour. Travel time without stops: four hours.

Highlights: *Fishermen's Life Museum, Clam Harbour Beach, Ship Harbour, Willy Krauch's smokehouse, Tangier gold, Taylor Head Provincial Park, Sheet Harbour, Port Dufferin, Sherbrooke Village, salmon fishing, Port Hilford Beach, Country Harbour ferry.*

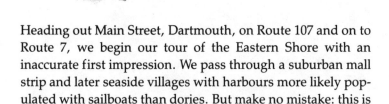

Heading out Main Street, Dartmouth, on Route 107 and on to Route 7, we begin our tour of the Eastern Shore with an inaccurate first impression. We pass through a suburban mall strip and later seaside villages with harbours more likely populated with sailboats than dories. But make no mistake: this is and has been, for the last 150 years, the realm of fishermen.

There is a beautiful shore and beaches close to the city (Lawrencetown and Martinique are both exceptional). But we are anxious to explore the more remote beaches farther down the shore.

134

We start our journey at a kind of symbolic juncture—the Fishermen's Life Museum at Jeddore Oyster Ponds.

The museum is a modest white-and-green-shingled cottage including grounds, a tiny fish shed, and a wharf. This is a "living" museum so our guide, in a long skirt and apron, welcomes us, like old friends, at the back stoop. She carefully removes a pan of molasses cookies from the kitchen woodstove and we get a taste while they're still soft and chewy.

A tour bus of senior citizens arrives. From the knowing glances they exchange with one another, we can tell that they

Fishermen's Life Museum, Jeddore Oyster Ponds

135

feel like they have just gone back to their childhood homes of sixty years ago.

This was the homestead for three generations of the Myers family. The museum staff shows us old photographs of all the relations.

What is so striking about this house is its understatement, how little these people needed to survive. The original house, which was 6.6 metres by 7.2 metres (22 feet by 24 feet), with an ell added later, sheltered over a dozen people. The bedroom, wedged between parlor and dining room, is barely the size of the bed itself. Thirteen daughters were born here. The family made do with one cast-iron stove, which, each fall, they moved back from the summer kitchen to heat the main house.

The fishing shed contains a wooden dory and other artifacts from the time when a bare livelihood was made fishing. Routinely on Monday morning, the Myers men would leave the house to the care of the women and row to Roger Island, where they had a camp. There they would spend the week hand-lining cod and haddock, not to return home until Saturday with their catch.

Looking at bygone fishermen's days with modern eyes, we can't help but compare their lives with our own. Life back then was far more physically challenging and materially unrewarding. Still, it's hard not to feel a little wistful for the astonishing everyday beauty: the orange daylily at their doorstep and the blue calm of Navy Pond, which they probably took for granted.

Back to Route 7, turn left and continue on for a few miles. Then turn right at Webbers "Log" General Store to (as the sign reads) "Clam Bay, Clam Harbour, Owl's Head, Little Harbour." With the windows rolled down we notice that the air has a frigid snap to it. We're travelling down a peninsula out to sea, and even the vegetation seems to shiver. The road is a bit boring, but the detour is worth it. Our destination is one of the most classically beautiful beaches in Nova Scotia.

Clam Harbour Beach is a generous swath of crystal sands with an infinity of swelling, breaking, surging, cresting, anything but stagnant waves. An exhilarating experience is guaranteed, and that is why this beach has been a favourite of people for generations, long before it was brought under the protection of the province.

The provincial park offers facilities: picnic tables, hiking trails, outdoor showers, a canteen, charcoal pits, change rooms, and (gratefully) flush toilets. A maze of ramps and boardwalks that protects the marram grass-covered dunes also makes the beach accessible to wheelchairs and baby strollers. Most visitors spend the whole day here.

In mid-August, Clam Harbour Beach holds its annual Sand-sculpting Contest. For the last fifteen years, thousands of enthusiastic people from the city have descended upon this beach with designs they've probably been dreaming about all winter: of giant locomotives, lobsters, mermaids, and, of course, castles.

Leaving the park, turn right to Owls Head and back to Route 7. The view opens up and the road switches back on Ship Harbour, a long, gentle, sheltered cove. The water is peppered with black buoys, which belong to the largest mussel farm in Nova Scotia. Because of the many sheltered coves on this road, there are lots of other aquacultured shellfish (under the telltale buoys) along this coast.

Strung from the buoys are 1.5- to 3-metre-long (5- to 10-foot-long) socks, which provide homes for the blue mussel spat. These mussels are exactly the same creatures as the wild ones we collect, which tenaciously hold on to rocks by their byssus threads. But because the cultivated mussels do not have to put energy into fighting the elements to survive, their shells are much thinner. To the consumer who buys shellfish by the pound, it means a much better value. These mussels are suspended off the ocean floor, so the meat is also free of pearls and grit. Local restaurants in the area serve fresh steamed mussels. The Nova Scotia Department of Fisheries has an Aquaculture Demonstration Centre in Ship Harbour. Here, native and European oysters, quahogs, and bay scallops are raised until they are large enough to be shipped out to local aquaculturists. During business hours there is a small display open to the public with videos, posters, and samples of gear such as mussel socks and lantern oyster nets. The centre enjoys a gorgeous view of Ship Harbour.

At East Ship Harbour and beyond there is a patch of signs offering a curious variety of wares and services: wooden buoys, smoked fish, pick-your-own strawberries, fish-your-own fish, blueberries, strawberries, cranberries, Lotto 49 tickets, handmade quilts, and outdoor sea-kayaking adventures.

Seven kilometres (4 miles) down the road in Tangier is Krauch's Smokehouse. It is off the main road with very well marked signs. Their Danish-style Nova maple and birch smoked salmon is world famous. Testimonials to this decorate the walls: from Craig Claiborne to the Prince of Wales. The perfume of smoke permeates the buildings, which cold smoke not only salmon but also eels, mackerel, and trout. Started in the 1950s by the late J. Willy Krauch (pronounced "Craw") the business is now run by his family, who lives across from the shop. Someone is usually around seven days of the week, twelve months a year.

Rockhounds please note: Tangier is also "gold country." Through the common rock outcroppings (slate and greywacke) that we see on the sides of the highway run quartz veins, which occasionally contain gold. In the middle of the nineteenth century, gold prospecting and some mining began in this area. It caught on like a brush fire and spread all down the Eastern Shore. Joseph Howe, journalist and later premier of Nova Scotia, described the event in 1860:

> A man stopping to drink at a brook, found a piece of gold shining among the pebbles over which the stream flowed. He picked it up, and searching found more. This was about half a mile to the eastward of the debouchment (mouth) of Tangier River.

Over the years, 26,000 ounces of gold were extracted. The mines opened up and closed down with the fluctuating price of gold. The mine entrance is visible from the road. Story has it that the Tangier Road was built on a bed of tailings from the old gold mine. Over the years people have bandied about the idea of digging up the road to reassess the rock with modern extraction methods.

There seems to be a pattern to this road, known as the Eastern Shore. Like a string of pearls, the road seems to be a collection of harbour communities. The shoreline is not made up of dramatic heights and drop-offs but has a gentle, consistent, scalloped edge. The road cuts across the top of most peninsulas, and we see from the head of each harbour a snapshot of the sea and islands framed by wooded sides. But we long for the whole picture! Visitors with time ask friendly residents where they go to see the open ocean.

If there ever was a place where the automobile had its limitations, it is on this shore. There are literally hundreds of islands, rocks, and ledges just beyond our reach from Tangier, Popes, Spry, Mushaboom, Sheet, and Beaver Harbours, through Quoddy and Necum Teuch Bay, Ecum Secum Inlet, Marie Joseph and Liscomb Harbours. We wish we had a boat.

With binoculars we see that the islands are a paradise for shorebirds. There are dense colonies of cormorants and common eider ducks. Leach's storm petrels, Arctic and common terns, black guillemots, osprey, and fox sparrows (rare in Nova Scotia) all nest here. In the spring and fall, migrating scoters, black ducks, old-squaws, and Canada geese fly through.

While watching the birds, we see curious dark patches bobbing amongst the waves. Seals are also at home here.

We can't reach the islands by car, but we can visit the next best thing—a rugged, windswept peninsula called Taylor Head that juts 7 kilometres (4 miles) into the Atlantic Ocean.

A government pamphlet explains the geology, flora, and fauna of the provincial park. Of particular interest are the "sand volcanoes" found in the rocks—small structures shaped in geologic time by the "early expulsion of water from the sediments due to increasing pressure from the overlying mud and sands."

The narrow gravel road takes us two-thirds of the way out Taylor Head to a parking lot, and then we're on our own. Here are picnic tables, pit toilets (but no drinking water), and a boardwalk, making the beach accessible to wheelchairs.

The marked trails loop through forests and barrens. Along the sand and cobbled shore they reveal startling views of Mushaboom Harbour and Spry Bay.

This is a wild place: home to reindeer lichen and pitcher plants, varying hares and mink. There is little sign of human habitation here except for a few unmarked graves and an abandoned cellar hole. Hardy lilac and rhubarb, planted 150 years ago by optimistic settlers, still grow next to rhodora and Indian pear.

Farther down the shore, nestled between two rivers (the East and the West) is Sheet Harbour, a town settled in 1784 by Loyalists and British veterans of the American Revolution. In its boom-town heyday, thousands of logs were floated down the rivers to feed four large lumber mills at the harbour. Two- and three-masted schooners up to 130 tons were built at the two major shipyards. In 1885, the first sulphite pulp mill in Canada was established here. On a hill overlooking the falls and the West River Bridge is the tourist bureau.

Travellers in a hurry to get to Sherbrooke can take the direct overland way on Route 7 to Port Dufferin. We prefer a much more scenic detour on a back shore road. Look for signs to Sober Island, Grant's Cove, and Beaver Harbour with a view of the islands and inlets. There are greenhouses at Grant's Cove with pick-your-own cranberries and Christmas trees. Sober Island was apparently named by a disgruntled surveyor who was not impressed by the local dry attitude toward intoxicants. The road comes out at Port Dufferin, where we turn right back onto Route 7 east.

Port Dufferin is a small, pretty community on Beaver Harbour named after the Marquis of Dufferin, Canada's governor general from 1872 to 1878. There are a number of interesting historic houses along the road. Built around 1850, their upstairs five-sided "Scottish dormers" look expectantly out to sea.

For a better look the harbour we take a small diversion past the motel down to Smiley's Point. There is a small Anglican church and a lovely cemetery. Amongst the blooming peonies and nasturtiums is one intriguing grave with a wrought-iron fence and a horizontal table stone that reads, "Sacred to the memory of AMELIA, Consort of Simon Fraser, who died the 28th of December, 1850, age 40 years old leaving numerous family to lament their irreparable loss."

The road between Port Dufferin and Sherbrooke is low key—lots of wooded areas with only an occasional view of the Atlantic. The tiny communities along the shore have tenaciously held on for fifty years through booms and busts in lumbering, shipbuilding, gold mining, and most recently, the terrible downturn in the fishery.

141

At Liscomb Mills we head inland. The Province of Nova Scotia owns and manages (and, word had it, is in the process of selling) the Liscomb Lodge, a luxurious yet rustic inn overhanging the banks of the St. Mary's River. Their specialty is planked salmon, a Mi'kmaq cooking technique where whole salmon are splayed open, lashed to a board, and baked golden next to an open fire. Originally the salmon would have come fresh out of the river but the fish served today, albeit delicious, are likely farm-raised.

Outside Liscomb the hills have been denuded of trees through clear-cutting practices. But hold on, it's 26 kilometres (16 miles) to Sherbrooke, the heart of our Eastern Shore trip.

The story of Sherbrooke is not unlike the story of many other villages all over the Maritimes, except for one thing: much of the original town survived into the 1960s, intact. Buildings constructed during the town's golden years, 100 years ago, may have been ignored and abandoned, but they were left standing. Sherbrooke's remoteness and lack of economic growth were factors in their salvation.

Sherbrooke simply never grew and evolved like other towns. It evaded the agonizing 1950s when whole downtowns of Georgian and Victorian architecture were modernized or bulldozed entirely to make way for flat, modern ones. Originally settled by the French in 1655 as a fur trading post, Fort Sainte Marie was captured by the English in 1669 and ignored for the next 100 years. As the waves of immigrants from Europe and New England demanded more and more land, English-speaking people were eventually granted land in the rich intervale known by 1815 as Sherbrooke.

Sherbrooke was remote in those days. The overland route was a long trudge on a rough path through the woods from Pictou or Musquodoboit. Settlers arriving by sea, on large ships from Halifax, were dropped off at the Head of the

Tide, where they transferred to a smaller boat for the trip upriver.

In the days of sail, and seemingly inexhaustible virgin timber stands, Sherbrooke thrived. The town exported planks, lath-wood, spars, oars, pickets, shingles, staves, handspikes, even firewood to Britain and the West Indies. Wooden ships were built to transport the wooden products, and the local economy provided work for woods workers, skilled mill-wrights, and sailmakers.

The professions to support a community opened up shop. The storekeeper, printer, blacksmith, druggist, and tailor moved in. People needed a church, school, doctor, court-house, and jail.

In 1861, gold was discovered here and all along the shore and a brief economic boom lasted twenty years.

After that, the town barely held its own. Until the restora-tion project eighty years later, visitors from the outside were mostly sports fishermen attracted to the salmon pools in the St. Mary's River.

Sherbrooke Village is not just a relic where the past is re-created for our entertainment. Peeking in the front window of the Cumminger Bros. General Store, grasping the hand-smoothed metal bars of the jail, posing in period costume in front of the ambrotype camera, we couldn't help but feel an added and poignant dimension.

Perhaps it has to do with the miniature scale of the place. We bring with us twentieth-century perceptions of time and space. (We think nothing of driving twenty minutes at 100 kilometres an hour, or 60 miles an hour, to pick up a few groceries.) Here, everything a person could possibly need in a lifetime was found within a five-minute stroll: a doctor to bring souls into the world, a school to educate them, a court to judge them, and a preacher to bury them. Down the road were neighbors who could turn trees into furniture, cloth into dresses, riverbank clay into bowls, and could even take your picture, for posterity.

Sherbrooke Village is not some brilliant archaeologists' "let's pretend" re-creation of what was. It *is*. The court that handed down fines to its wayward citizens 100 years ago is still in session. The jail lockup was used into the 1960s. The Presbyterian church continues to minister to the spiritual needs of the great-great-great grandchildren of the original villagers. This village, where private citizens dwell amongst museum buildings, is alive.

After leaving Sherbrooke Village, Route 7 continues to follow the river valley north.

The first part of the drive closely follows the salmon pools (Flat Rock Pool, Oak Tree Pool). Fishermen up to their waists in water gracefully cast, in what seems to be slow motion, their 15-metre (50-foot) fly lines.

There are two places to explore the river firsthand. One stop is at a lovely treed picnic park just outside Sherbrooke. Its sheltered tables are handy in inclement weather.

Another spot is at the bridge that spans the St. Mary's on the road to Waternish. Rushing rapids are contained within canyon walls.

Travellers may continue on Route 7 to the main road, Highway 104, turning east to Cape Breton or west to New Glasgow and Halifax.

Another option is to venture, for a few more hours, along the coast. This route includes an interesting ferry ride. Turn right just past the sign to Waternish and Glenelg at Stillwater on Route 211 to Port Bickerton and the Country Harbour ferry. A sign tells us whether or not the ferry is running.

In the next 24 kilometres (14 miles) to Port Hilford the road passes through mixed forest next to a succession of lakes, rather unimaginatively named: Sixth, Fifth, Fourth, Third, and Second. This chain of lakes, ending in Indian Harbour Lake, appears to have been the original route of the St. Mary's River before the flow was disrupted by glacier movements 10,000 years ago.

At Port Hilford, we return to the North Atlantic, where the salt air is sharp and invigorating. A rubble bar has cut off the fresh water of Indian Harbour Lake from the crashing surf of Indian Harbour.

Stay on Route 211 to Port Bickerton, a scenic fishing village. The road cuts inland for 7 kilometres (4 miles) of a non-stop bog called Squinces Glades. A glade is defined as an "open space surrounded by woods." We think this is an overly optimistic description of this place (and who was Squince?). The bedrock is covered by a thin layer of stony soil, which, combined with poor drainage, allows only the sparsest of vegetation to grow here. But it is reported that deer like this area in winter because it receives considerably less snowfall than elsewhere on the coast.

We are relieved to dip down into the woods at the entrance to the Country Harbour ferry. We park our car in line and with a little time on our hands poke around Lucas Beach and the pond just down from the ferry.

The ferry leaves, and from the middle of the harbour, looking up at the high cliffs on each side, we notice that this is an impressive body of water. A huge fault in the earth's crust has created this deep, 17-kilometre-long (10-mile-long) harbour.

The green hills have a raw, haunting beauty, and on the west side is a promontory called Mount Misery. Travelling across we can't help but notice that the boat seems to be ferrying us from nowhere to nowhere. There is little evidence of man here.

This area was settled, albeit briefly, by a regiment of the last royal governor of North Carolina. Each man who had defended the crown in the Revolutionary War was allotted land, tools, materials, and provisions for three years. On Christmas of 1783, 900 men, women, and children sailed into Country Harbour and landed at a place that was later to be christened Mount Misery. A town plot, a glebe, a road, and a school lot as well as 4,750 acres were set aside for them across the harbour at Stormont.

Coming from the southern United States where the climate was considerably more hospitable, they did not fair well. One-third of them died that winter of the cold and scurvy. Many of the survivors left and the surveyed town was never built. Some people did make homes for themselves, and their descendants still remain in the area.

Ending our tour of the Eastern Shore at Country Harbour is somehow satisfying. Ferrying across this extraordinarily beautiful, isolated inlet we contemplate the tiny coastal harbour communities we've travelled through, Jeddore Oyster Ponds and Sherbrooke, the town that stood still. We think of the roaring surf at Clam Harbour, Taylor Head, and Port Hilford. If there is a continuing thread in the road we have just travelled, it is that man has hardly made a scratch in nature's great plan for the Eastern Shore of Nova Scotia.

On the east side of the harbour, disembark, following the road to the corner, where we turn left to Goshen and Antigonish.

In the Area

Antigonish-Eastern Shore Tourist Association: 902-845-2450, 902-889-3353

Fishermen's Life Museum (Jeddore Oyster Ponds): 902-889-2053

Aquaculture Demonstration Centre (Ship Harbour): 902-845-2991

J. Willy Krauch and Sons Ltd. (Tangier): 902-772-2188

Nova Scotia Department of Natural Resources—Parks
(Musquodoboit Harbour): 902-889-2332

Sherbrooke Village (Sherbrooke): 902-522-2400

Country Harbour ferry information (Goldboro):
902-424-5433

12 ~

Enchanted Valley:

The Margaree

Crossing the Canso Causeway: Take Highway 105 toward Baddeck for about 65 kilometres (40 miles). Turn left (before Baddeck) at exit 7 on the Cabot Trail and head toward Middle River. Follow the trail for about 25 kilometres (15 miles) to the sign for Lakes O'Law Provincial Picnic Park.

From Sydney: Take Route 125 west to North Sydney, to the Trans-Canada Highway (Highway 105) west to exit 7. The road goes to Margaree Harbour and follows the shore to Inverness for 85 kilometres (50 miles). Travel time without stops: two hours.

Highlights: *Lakes O'Law, the Normaway Inn, the Margaree Fish Culture Station, Big Intervale, Margaree River, a quiltmaker, Margaree Salmon Museum, Father Coady, Margaree Harbour, Broad Cove Marsh.*

Most travellers "from away" don't give themselves nearly enough time to explore Cape Breton Island properly. Pressed for time, with a day or two to spare, they naturally seek out the most publicized and dramatic road—the Cabot Trail. This is a shame because Cape Breton deserves to be examined square inch by square inch.

Our road is less travelled. It loops back and forth though Inverness County, following the meandering river valleys and seaside bluffs. It does include short sections of the famous "trail."

Lakes O'Law is spellbinding. Behold miniature lakes of crystal water with the perfectly mirrored visages of the Three Sisters, mountains that rise 425 metres (1,400 feet) off the valley floor. Welcome to the Margaree.

Picnic tables are a few paces from the shimmering water. Setting out lunch, it's easy to disturb the loons who cry in eerie protest, their wingtips clack-clacking the water as they take flight.

Under the water are cages of live, swimming salmon, which biologists are trying to reintroduce into the lake.

Lakes O'Law is more a collection of ponds than lakes, fed by ten little brooks. At the south end of the park we hear one of them. The energetic sound of tumbling granite pebbles is irresistible.

A privately owned campground down the road rents canoes for exploring the mysterious other side of the lake. They also have go-carts and a restaurant.

There are many more than three sisters. The road courses between dozens and dozens of overlapping, deeply gouged, green, hardwood-covered hills. It's hard to know whether to call these 340- to 450-metre (1,200- to 1,500-foot) peaks hills or mountains.

Looking up from the valley floor, they look like a series of separate, freestanding peaks. But interestingly, there is only one mountain—a giant, high, flat rock mass called the Northern Plateau. It stretches from Margaree in the south to the tip of the island at Cape North; from Presqu'ile on the west coast to Cape Smoky on the east coast.

What we see are the eroded edges of the plateau. The straight-edged escarpments have been softened by weather and upheavals in the earth's crust. Water pooling in the highlands cascaded down the rock face, gnawing away crevices and shaping the hills. Eventually the jagged rock shoulders of the plateau were softened with a luxurious growth of boreal forest.

It is hard to explain why the Margaree is so enchanting. Some days the sunlight is so sharp and bright that the hills seem to vibrate facets of green. On other days they are swaddled in an ethereal blue haze. There is a healthy flowing vibrancy to the forest. Everywhere mountain streams babble noisily through hearty stands of rock maple and yellow and white birch. In the fall there is the incredible alchemy in the woods: the transformation of green to scarlet, orange, and yellow. In winter, when the leaves are matted on the forest floor under a pack of white snow, cross-country-ski enthusiasts glide for miles on old woods roads. The view of the Margaree Valley, from the top of the plateau, opened up by the leafless trees, is glorious.

Leaving the park, travel a few miles down the road, turn right, and cross a bridge to curiously titled Egypt Road (near Nile Brook). According to one source, the name has biblical significance. Irad Hart, who settled the Margaree in the early 1800s, divided his land amongst his four sons. A fifth son, Joseph, obtained a grant of land in another area, and it was said that Joseph "had gone down to Egypt."

Follow Egypt Road for the next 5 kilometres (3 miles) to Margaree Valley. This used to be farmland. Typically, many fields have grown up in sticker bushes and "stinkin' Willie" (wild roses and tansy ragwort). Now those who farm do it more because they like the lifestyle, and they sustain it with income from off the farm.

The beautiful white pine-lined driveway on the left leads to the Normaway Inn. Built in 1928 by George McPherson, a local boy who made his fortune in the gold mines of Colorado, it was originally used as a summer retreat for clergymen. Designed by a New York architect to guarantee maximum privacy for each guest, it was reputed to have cost $85,000 (indeed a fortune in those days) to build. The 1929 crash turned McPherson's fortunes around, and soon he was offering shelter and victuals to the public.

Today the inn offers old-fashioned comfort (fieldstone fireplace and wicker rocking chair-style) and wholesome country food to families who have been visiting the Margaree for generations. Newcomers, of course, are also welcome.

The Normaway is not open in the winter. Visitors who come to the area for the exceptionally fine cross-country skiing stay at Heart of Harts guest home in nearby Northeast Margaree.

Near Ross Road, the resourceful Wesley Burton family is taking advantage of the sugar maple stands on their property. Stop at the sign reading "Burton's Pure Maple Syrup."

At the end of Egypt Road turn right. We stop at Macpherson's Lucky Dollar Store for a few provisions. In this area we especially need some insect repellent (just ask for "fly dope"). This seems to be a good place for hanging out, so we ask for directions (e.g., How do we get to the fish hatchery and the Big Intervale?). We note a gentle Gaelic lilt in the speech here and questions that require an affirmative are answered with a deeply inhaled "yeahhh."

We wonder why there are so many Margarees: Northeast Margaree, Southwest Margaree, Margaree Valley, Margaree Harbour, Margaree Centre, East Margaree, Upper Margaree. Some are bona fide original names. But the story goes that some brilliant civil servant decided it would be less confusing to tourists to change the remaining non-Margarees, such as Cranton Section, to Margaree Centre, and Frizzleton to Margaree Valley.

Margareeers have dealt with the burden of too many Margarees by dispensing with the nomenclature altogether. Asking directions on how to get from the Lucky Dollar to Lake Ainslie, we were told, "Turn right at the Northeast, follow the Trail to the Forks, and turn left up to the Southwest."

Continue on through the village of Margaree Valley, past the post office to a Y in the road. Take the road to the right for 1.25 kilometres (3/4 mile) and turn left at the next road. It's a half mile to the Federal Department of Fisheries and Ocean's Margaree Fish Culture Station, commonly known since 1902 as the "Hatchery." The gushing waters of Ingram Brook feed a maze of holding ponds, providing the living medium for salmon at various stages in their development: parr, fry, smolts, grilse, and adults. It is a fascinating place, especially for children with a goldfish at home, to observe schools of fish darting through the water a few feet away.

Fish biologists visit river pools to net large fish, which are trucked back to the station and milked for their eggs. The adults are returned to the river and the eggs are raised in the protection of the hatchery until they can be safely reintroduced back into their river habitat.

A new interpretation centre sits high on the bank of the babbling, rocky brook known as the Northeast Margaree River. This is our first access to one branch of the mighty Margaree that we will be trailing for a good part of our journey. Note the fascinating rock face of pink crystalline gypsum just up the river.

At this point you may choose to take a 12-kilometre (7-mile) diversion (24 kilometres or 14 miles there and back) on a gravel road up to Big Intervale. We think of it as the hidden jewel of the Cabot Trail and well worth the time.

Intervale is a word commonly used in these parts to describe the flat area between two mountains. It is an archaic form of the word *interval*, which roughly means a space between two objects. An interval is also an intermission in time between events. Travelling this beautiful road, which threads its way between mountain and mountain, will indeed give us reason to pause.

To reach Big Intervale, turn right at the hatchery gates and take the next left at the T in the road leading from Margaree Valley. Travel a few miles to the base of conical-shaped Sugar Loaf Mountain (named after an ancient way of molding sugar). This mountain, a 5-kilometre-long and 450-metre-high (3-mile-long and 1,500-foot-high) freestanding granite mass, was fragmented from the main plateau.

The west side of Sugar Loaf is defined by the northeast branch of the Margaree River. This side is accessible only by foot. An old woods path runs down the river canyon and is an outstanding hiking path. It's called the Black Rock Trail and extends from Portree to the Salmon Camp at Big Intervale.

Our road follows the western side of Sugar Loaf, a narrow valley created by Ingram Brook. We drive 7 kilometres (4 miles) through a heavily wooded mountain pass to the intervale, which opens wide. At one time these fields were all under cultivation, but now they are mostly grown up in small spruce.

The community on this side of the river is called Kingross, after the original settler, Angus Ross, who made such a success of his life here that he became known as "King Ross." (We suspect there is more to this story.)

We cross the iron bridge into the community. All it consists of is a few houses and a place name on the map. But Big Intervale is not wilderness. The area is well known to residents and sports fishermen from all over North America. This is the beginning of the scheduled part of the Margaree River.

On a hot day, we slide down the bank to cool off in the rushing brook. This river may seem tame in summer, but when the melting snow and spring rains combine, it often jumps its banks. Recently the swollen stream tore the underpinnings right out from under the Big Intervale Bridge.

Just past the iron bridge is an old farmhouse and barn on which is painted a 5-by-5-metre (15-by-15-foot) wedding-ring-pattern quilt. Anne Morrell Robinson is a quiltmaker and fibre artist whose one-of-a-kind quilts are more likely to adorn a wall or gallery than a bed. Her complex appliquéd images are inspired by her natural environment: the bald eagles that fly overhead, her garden, vegetables, the river, and even salmon fishing. Because of her passion for fishing, biking, hiking, and skiing, it's best to call the day before to make an appointment.

Anne's sons Ezra and Amish know these woods like the backs of their hands and are available to do backcountry guiding, either on foot or mountain bike.

Back down the 12 kilometres (7 miles) of gravel to the turnoff to the hatchery, we get a different perspective, and it doesn't seem like the same road at all. Turn right, toward the hatchery again, and follow the road to Portree, where we cross the Northeast Margaree River at Ross's Bridge. In season, fishermen will be working the Ross Pool and East Findlay Rock Pool. Travel a few miles through the valley and up Boarsback (or Hogsback) Hill to the next intersection. Turn left toward Margaree Valley, past the elementary school, and over the Cranton Bridge. On a hot afternoon we are tempted to join families splashing around in the river. Teenagers dive off the bridge.

Turn right to Northeast Margaree and the Margaree Salmon Museum. The museum is housed in the old wood-framed Rossville School and has none of the cold professionalism of a city institution. Rather it is a collection of salmon memorabilia that has been lovingly collected, donated, and preserved by the community.

The community consists of local people, members of the Margaree Anglers Association, including Ms. Frances Hart, who has been the curator since 1966, and also anglers from all over the world. These people have, for over 100 years, made an annual pilgrimage to the Margaree, not only for the fish but also for the serene rhythm of life and to breathe in the fresh mountain air.

Angling for early morning salmon

Housed in the museum are hundreds of objects, including a rare Royal Doulton figurine of a leaping salmon called "Rouge Flambe" with a bloodred glaze. It was donated by the late Ross Taylor, whose wife, Isabel, was the first president of the association. The museum also contains an extensive library of old books in a glass-fronted oak bookcase (with titles such as *Secrets of Salmon Fishermen*) and framed poems and watercolours donated by the artists. The yellowed photographs and postcards tell poignant tales of the old days: of smiling guides and anglers and large fish that stretched from a man's waist to the ground.

There are wooden rods of apple, bamboo, and rock maple, and hundreds and hundreds of flies, rods, and reels.

Some are framed behind glass, others are mounted in tin boxes or tacked to the wall. Every one of them is a fish story in itself. Each has been kindly donated and is accompanied by an often hand-written note of explanation.

Back on the Cabot Trail, travel east through Emerald to Margaree Forks. At Emerald, the Northeast Margaree River makes a ninety-degree to the west. At the Forks it joins forces with the Southwest Margaree River. Together they make another ninety-degree and flow to the sea under a new united name, the Margaree River. Strangely, this river flows in a direction almost completely opposite to that of the Northeast Margaree, which we followed in Big Intervale.

Of Margaree Forks, J. L. MacDougall wrote in 1922 in his *History of Inverness County, Nova Scotia*:

Here the North East and South West branches of the Margaree River meet and embrace on their joyful way to the salt sea. The sea is nine miles distant from the "Forks" and it is the combined volume of those two river branches that gives unto this favored place its everlasting health and hope.

The Forks is unusual in that it was settled by Irish rather than Scottish immigrants. In 1815 Myles McDaniel arrived, and gradually others came. Their names were Tompkins, Doyle, Coakly, McGarry, Carrolls, and Coady.

There is a tourist bureau here, and nearby a public library dedicated to one of the Forks' native sons, Father Moses Michael Coady. Born into a family of farmers in 1882, he became a priest, teacher, and eventually director of extension at Saint Francis Xavier University in Antigonish.

Observing the economic suffering of fishermen, farmers, and miners in Cape Breton, Coady came to believe that the key to solving their problems was adult education and cooperative group effort. Study circles were organised in communities for people to discuss their economic woes. Often cooperatives and credit unions were formed during these meetings. Coady helped organise the Nova Scotia Teachers' Union and the United Maritime Fishermen.

Along with his cousin and mentor, Father J. J. "Jimmy" Tompkins, and his assistant, A. B. Macdonald, Coady created "the Antigonish Movement." Coady's translated speeches reverberated into the Third World. In the 1950s, adult educators and social activists started coming to Antigonish to study. In 1959 the Coady International Institute was established as a training centre for people from Latin America, Africa, and Asia.

Follow the road down to Margaree Harbour, a scenic collection of houses and wharves where the river merges with the sea. Just down from the lighthouse is a good swimming beach with fine sand dunes, protected by a triangular concrete-block breakwater. Look for the monster rock covered with birds' nests. To the right, there's a wonderful view up the coast toward Chéticamp with no less than seven rises superimposed over one another.

Back to the main road, we follow Route 219 south toward Inverness. The road veers back and forth from the shoreline. From the cliffs the view is breathtaking, and we see two gentle moon-shaped beaches along the way at Whale Cove and Chimney Corner. Both are havens for swimmers.

The gravel turnoff to Chimney Corner Beach is unmarked, but it is the only public road along this stretch. A freshwater stream cuts across this beach, making it more fun for puddling about. A dramatic, high, rocky cliff extends out into the water, and embedded between the sandstone and shale are black strata of coal. In fact, coal was mined here at the turn of the century, but the mine was closed down. The seam stretches under the water, and mining it was a dangerous game because the potential for flooding was always present.

Offshore is Margaree Island. We prefer its alternate nomenclature—Sea Wolf Island.

In Dunvegan there is a cairn dedicated to Angus Lewis Macdonald, who was born here in 1890. He was premier of Nova Scotia from 1933 to 1940 and 1945 to 1954, when he died in office. A fine orator, he was elected during the Great Depression and introduced old-age pensions and relief for the unemployed. He was said never to have forgotten his Dunvegan roots and was much loved by all Nova Scotians. A bridge crossing Halifax Harbour is named in his honor.

Just down the road, we cross the bridge and leave Route 19 by turning right on the gravel road toward Broad Cove Marsh. This road is stunning and definitely not to be missed: 110-metre-high (350-foot-high) cliffs with cascading mountain brooks, coal grey beaches, and 180 degrees of ocean views.

We get out, but don't want to venture too close to the edge. Hunkering down next to the car with a pair of binoculars, we gaze out to sea—and see whales breaching and diving.

No one speeds along here, and we hope not to meet any other vehicles, especially large camper vans, coming from the opposite direction. Some people say that this road is what the Cabot Trail was like fifty years ago: not quite two lanes wide with a shoulder that can drop automobiles unceremoniously to the rocks below.

Unfortunately we have not followed the advice of fifty years ago, which is still given to travellers on the trail. We are encouraged to "travel clockwise," which guarantees that in the event that we meet another vehicle, headlight to headlight, we would have the preferred, inside lane. Our cliffside drive is only a few miles long and we hope this will not be an issue!

Broad Cove Chapel, a church with a permanent band-stand in the backyard, is the scene every August of the "Broad Cove Scottish Concert." It is billed as "the largest of its kind," and "not just a parish event, it is a Celtic happening!" Check with the tourist bureau for exact dates.

Thousands of people flock to this event, which runs from mid-afternoon until dark, with a lively "party" atmosphere. It's best to arrive early and bring a blanket or fold-up chairs and a lunch. There is plenty of local talent: fiddlers, pipers, step dancers, and Gaelic singers as well as stars such as Buddy MacMaster from Judique. Much of the choral work will be in the Gaelic language. *Am Braighe,* a newspaper published out of Mabou, describes Gaelic as

a Celtic language closely related to Irish. Gaelic language and culture was established in Scotland by colonists from Ireland in the fourth century A.D. It was the language spoken by immigrants from the Highlands and Islands of Scotland to Canada and is still spoken by their descendants today. Gaelic language learning is presently flourishing internationally.

The sound of the fiddlers' reels, accompanied by kilted dancers and sweet Gaelic singing, evokes strong emotions, even in those born far from the Highlands.

Our journey ends at Inverness, but there is a whole island of more Cape Breton beauty and Gaelic culture to explore.

Travellers headed back to the causeway are lucky. The Mabou Highlands rival the Margaree for sheer beauty.

To return to the Cabot Trail, either double back to Route 19 to Margaree Forks or better still, travel south to Kenloch, North Ainslie, Scotsville, up to Southwest Margaree to Margaree Forks. Turn right to Baddeck. For an alternate route to Chéticamp and the Cabot Trail, cross Doyles Bridge to see the other side of the Margaree, picking up the trail at Belle Côte, across the river mouth from Margaree Harbour.

In the Area

Burton, Wesley (Egypt Road): 902-248-2588

Coady and Tompkins Memorial Library (Margaree Forks): 902-248-2821

Heart of Harts (Northeast Margaree): 902-248-2765

Macpherson's Lucky Dollar Store (Margaree Valley): 902-248-2541

Margaree Fish Culture Station (Margaree Valley): 902-248-2845

Margaree Forks Tourist Bureau (Margaree Forks): 902-248-2803

Margaree Salmon Museum (Northeast Margaree): 902-248-2848

Robinson, Anne Morrell, Quilts and Other Comforts (Big Intervale): 902-248-2466

The Normaway Inn (Northeast Margaree): 902-248-2987

Bibliography

Books

Baldwin, Douglas. *Land of the Red Soil: A Popular History of Prince Edward Island.* Charlottetown: Ragweed Press, 1990.

Blakeley, Phyllis Ruth. *Nova Scotia: A Brief History.* Toronto: J. M. Dent and Sons, 1955.

Calder, Doris. *All Our Born Days: A Lively History of New Brunswick's Kingston Peninsula.* Sackville: Percheron Press, Tantramar Publishing Ltd., 1984.

Clarke, George Frederick. *Expulsion of the Acadians.* Fredericton: University Press of New Brunswick, 1955.

Clough, Katherine. *Wildflowers of Prince Edward Island.* Charlottetown: Ragweed Press, 1992.

Connell, Allison. *A View of Woodstock: Historic Homes of the Nineteenth Century.* Fredericton: New Ireland Press, 1988.

Cunningham, Scott. *Coastal Paddling Routes in Nova Scotia.* Self-published, n.d.

Dawson, Joan. *The Mapmaker's Eye: Nova Scotia Through Early Maps.* Halifax: Nimbus Publishing Ltd. and Nova Scotia Museum, 1988.

Dennis, Clara. *Down in Nova Scotia: My Own, My Native Land.* Toronto: The Ryerson Press, 1934.

Dunn, Charles W. *Highland Settler: A Portrait of the Scottish Gael in Cape Breton and Eastern Nova Scotia.* (Originally published by University of Toronto Press, 1953.) Wreck Cove: Breton Books, 1991.

Erskine, John. *In Forest and Field.* Halifax: Nova Scotia Museum, 1976.

Ferguson, Laing. *The Fossil Cliffs of Joggins*. The Nova Scotia Museum, 1988.

Finley, A. Gregg, editor. *The Loyalists: A Catalogue Featuring Selected Pieces of Loyalist History from the Collections of the New Brunswick Museum*. Saint John: New Brunswick Museum, 1975.

Ganong, W. F. *A Monograph of Historic Sites in the Province of New Brunswick*. (Originally published 1899.) St. Stephen: Print 'N' Press Ltd., 1983.

Grant, John N. *The Development of Sherbrooke Village to 1880*. Halifax: Nova Scotia Museum, 1972.

Hamilton, William B. *The Nova Scotia Traveller*. Toronto: Macmillan, 1981.

Kaulback, Ruth E. *Historic Saga of Leheve [LaHave]*. Petite Rivière: Self-published, 1971.

Ketchem, Bradford W., Jr., Jay Paris, Carmi Zona-Paris, and the editors of *Walking* magazine. *Walking Nova Scotia: The Doer's and Dreamer's Complete Guide to Canada's Walking Province*. Boston: Walking, Inc., 1993.

Lakes, Salt Marshes, and the Narrow Green Strip: Some Historic Buildings in Dartmouth and Halifax County's Eastern Shore. Halifax: Heritage Trust of Nova Scotia, 1979.

Lawson, Patricia M., Gail Farnsworth, and M. Anne Hartley. *The Nackawic Bend: 200 Years of History*. Town of Nackawic, 1985.

Lebreton, Clarence. *Yesterday in Acadia: Scenes from the Acadian Historical Village*. Caraquet: Acadian Historical Village, 1987.

Lonngstreth, T. Morris. *To Nova Scotia: The Sunrise Province*. Toronto: The Ryerson Press, 1947 (originally published 1935).

MacDonald, Florence M. *Sherbrooke . . . As I Remember It*. Self-published 1987.

MacDougall, J. L. *History of Inverness County*. Belleville: Mika, 1972 (originally published 1922).

Malpeque and Its People. Malpeque Historical Society, self-published, 1982.

Maritime Dykelands: The 350-Year Struggle. Department of Agriculture and Marketing, Province of Nova Scotia, 1987.

Bibliography

Miller, Craig T., and G. Clinton Milligan. *A Guide to the Geology, Landscapes, and Mineral Resources of Nova Scotia*. Halifax: Dalhousie University, Department of Geology.

A Natural History of Kings County, Nova Scotia. Wolfville: The Blomidon Naturalists Society, 1992.

Natural History of Nova Scotia. Halifax: Nova Scotia Museum, 1984.

Penney, Allen. *Houses of Nova Scotia: An Illustrated Guide to Architectural-Style Recognition*. Halifax: Formac Publishing Co. and the Nova Scotia Museum, 1989.

Rayburn, Alan. *Geographical Names of Prince Edward Island: Toponymy Study 1*. Ottawa: Supply and Services Canada, 1978.

Ricker, Jackson. *Historical Sketches of Glenwood and the Argyles, Yarmouth County, Nova Scotia*. Halifax: McCurdy Print, 1941.

Robertson, Marion. *Red Earth: Tales of the Micmacs with an Introduction to the Customs and Beliefs of the Micmac Indians*. Halifax: Nova Scotia Museum, 1969.

Roland, Albert E. *Geological Background and Physiography of Nova Scotia*. Halifax: Nova Scotia Museum, 1982.

Ross, Daphne. *Seascapes of Prince Edward Island*. Charlottetown: Ragweed Press, 1992.

St. Andrews Heritage Handbook: A Homeowner's Guide to Exterior Renovation and Maintenance of Local Buildings. St. Andrews Civic Trust, 1980.

Spicer, Stanley T. *Sails of Fundy: The Schooners and Square-Riggers of the Parrsboro Shore*. Hantsport: Lancelot Press, 1984.

Thomas, George C. *Margaree*. Margaree Harbour: Harbour Lights Press, 1980.

Thurston, Harry. *Tidal Life: A Natural History of the Bay of Fundy*. Camden East: Camden House Publishing, 1990.

Townshend, Adele. *Ten Farms Become a Town: A History of Souris, Prince Edward Island, 1700-1920*. The Town of Souris, 1986.

Tracy, Nicholas. *A Cruising Guide to the Bay of Fundy and the St. John River: Including Passamaquoddy Bay and the Southwestern Shore of Nova Scotia*. Fredericton: Goose Lane Editions, 1992.

Trask, Deborah. *Life How Short, Eternity How Long: Gravestone Carving and Carvers in Nova Scotia.* Halifax: Nova Scotia Museum, 1978.

Trueman, Stuart. *An Intimate History of New Brunswick.* Toronto: McClelland and Stewart Ltd., 1970.

Tufts, Robie W. *Birds of Nova Scotia.* Halifax: Nimbus Publishing Ltd. and the Nova Scotia Museum, 1986 (first edition 1961).

Walker, Willa. *No Hay Fever and a Railway: Summers in St. Andrews, Canada's First Seaside Resort.* Fredericton: Goose Lane Editions, 1989.

Wilbur, Richard, and Ernest Wentworth. *Silver Harvest: The Fundy Weirmen's Story.* Fredericton: Goose Lane Editions, 1986.

Wright, Esther Clark. *The Saint John River.* Toronto: McClelland and Stewart Ltd., 1949.

Wright, Esther Clark. *The Saint John River and Its Tributaries.* Self-published, 1966.

Periodicals and Pamphlets

The Island Magazine, various issues. Charlottetown, Prince Edward Island Heritage Foundation.

Mullen, Eric, and Millie Evans. *Our Land and Water.* Charlottetown: Prince Edward Island Department of the Environment, 1979.

Pentz, Donald R. *Risser's Beach Salt Marsh Trail.* Halifax, Nova Scotia: Department of Lands and Forests, n.d.

Index

BRIDGES, DAMS and
  DYKES (*cont.*)
  World's longest covered
  bridge, Hartland,
  38–39

CANTEENS and
  LODGING
Algonquin Hotel,
  St. Andrews, 12
Carrefour de la Mer,
  Caraquet, 48
Coffee Merchant,
  Wolfville, 103
Dutchman Cheese
  Shop and "Deel"
  Tearoom, Upper
  Economy, 85
Evangeline Motel,
  Grand Pre, 102
Eveleigh Hotel,
  Evandale, 25–26
Heart of Harts,
  Northeast Margaree,
  151
Island View Canteen,
  Browns Flat,
  24
Kitchen Witch, Long
  River, 71
Liscomb Lodge,
  Liscomb Mills, 142
Macleod's Canteen,
  Green Bay, 127,
  128–129

Mactaquac Provincial
  Park, Mactaquac,
  31–32
Matthews House, Souris,
  62
Normaway Inn,
  Northeast Margaree,
  150–151
P.E.I. Preserves
  Company, New
  Glasgow, 70
CITIES. *See* PROVINCES,
  CITIES and TOWNS
CRAFT and LIVING
  HISTORY SITES
Acadian Historical
  Village, Caraquet,
  45–48
Covey Island Boatworks,
  Petite Riviere, 128
New Dublin Water
  Craft, Dublin Shore,
  130
Anne Morrell Robinson
  quilts, Big Intervale,
  153–154
Sherbrooke Village,
  Sherbrooke, 143–144
Sunbury Shores Art
  and Nature Centre,
  St. Andrews, 9–10

DAMS and DYKES. *See*
  BRIDGES, DAMS and
  DYKES

Lucy Maud Montgomery
Birthplace, New
London, 71
Mount Misery, Country
Harbour, 145–146
Planters' Elm, Wolfville,
97–98
Prescott House, Starrs
Point, 105
Saint John the Evangelist
Roman Catholic Parish
church, Johnville,
40
Saint Paul's Anglican
Church, Greenwich,
24–25
St. James United
Church, Great Village,
84
St. Mary's Roman
Catholic Church,
Indian River, 75
St. Stephen's Church,
Tusket, 116
Ste. Anne's Church, Ste.
Anne du Ruisseau, 117
Marie Babin Surette
tombstone, Surette's
Island, 117
Telegraph Hill,
Bayswater, 21
Town Point Cemetery,
Chebogue, 112–114
Trinity Anglican Church,
Kingston, 27

Yankee Hill cemetery,
French River, 71–72

ISLANDS, PENINSULAS
and RIVERS
Acadian Peninsula,
42–53
Campobello Island,
4–6
Cape Breton Island,
148–160
Caton's Island, 23–24
Chebogue Point,
110–114
Deer Island, 6–8
Kingston Peninsula,
16–27
LaHave Islands,
129–130
Lameque Island, 50–52
Minister's Island,
13–14
Miscou Island, 52
Morris Island, 117
Prince Edward Island,
57–80
Rocco Point, 117
Sluice Point, 116–117
Spencers Island,
91–92
St. John River, 16–27,
29–41
Surette's Island,
116–117
Tusket Islands, 112

PROVINCES, CITIES and
TOWNS (*cont.*)

RIVERS. *See* ISLANDS,
PENINSULAS and
RIVERS

SCENIC SITES and
WILDLIFE
SHOPS. *See* FARMERS'
MARKETS and
SHOPS

Other titles in the Country Roads series:

Country Roads of Connecticut and Rhode Island
Country Roads of Hawaii
Country Roads of Illinois, second edition
Country Roads of Indiana
Country Roads of Kentucky
Country Roads of Massachusetts
Country Roads of Michigan, second edition
Country Roads of New Hampshire
Country Roads of New York
Country Days in New York City
Country Roads of North Carolina
Country Roads of Ohio
Country Roads of Oregon
Country Roads of Pennsylvania
Country Roads of Quebec
Country Roads of Tennessee
Country Roads of Vermont
Country Roads of Virginia
Country Roads of Washington

All books are $9.95 at bookstores.
Or order directly from the publisher (add $3.00
shipping & handling for direct orders):
Country Roads Press
P.O. Box 286
Castine, Maine 04421
Toll-free phone number: **800-729-9179**